MW01087651

22 DAYS TO A GREATER UNDERSTANDING OF GOD'S WORD

Thy
Word

A Devotional Commentary on
Psalm 119

David A. Chapman, D.Min.

Thy Word

David Chapman, D.Min.

Printed in the United States of America. All rights reserved under International Copyright Law. Contents and/or cover may not be reproduced in whole or in part in any form without the expressed written consent of the Publisher.

All Bible quotations are from the King James Version unless otherwise noted.

Copyright © 2019

TRU Publishing
1726 S. 1st Ave.
Safford, Arizona 85546

Table of Contents

Introduction 4

The Author and His Trials 5

Nine Hebrew Words for the Word of God 7

Day 1 16

Day 2 21

Day 3 26

Day 4 32

Day 5 37

Day 6 42

Day 7 47

Day 8 52

Day 9 57

Day 10 63

Day 11 69

Day 12 75

Day 13 81

Day 14 87

Day 15 93

Day 16 99

Day 17 105

Day 18 111

Day 19 116

Day 20 122

Day 21 128

Day 22 134

Introduction

Psalm 119 consists of 22 stanzas, or paragraphs, of eight verses each. These stanzas correspond to the 22 letters in the Hebrew alphabet. Every verse of each stanza begins with the same corresponding Hebrew letter.

Also unique to the Psalm is the beautiful descriptiveness of the Word of God. In the Psalm, there are nine different words used for the Holy Scripture, with each having a unique Hebrew word in the original. We will start by looking at these nine Hebrew words and defining them. Throughout this prayer devotional we will continually refer to these Hebrew words.

Luke 4:4 But Jesus answered him, saying, "It is written, 'Man shall not live by bread alone, but by every word of God.'"

Not long after I was saved and shortly after God called me into the ministry of His Word, I was led by the Spirit to pray through Psalm 119 in its entirety every evening. I did this for approximately one year. As a result, I experienced much revelation of God's Word in answer to those prayers. While time constraints may limit one from praying through all 176 verses each day, the Psalm is perfectly laid out to pray one stanza (8 verses) each day over a 22-day period. Ideally, this should be done more than once.

Note: The King James Version of the Bible has been used when quoting Psalm 119 due to its beautiful and poetic wording in the Psalms, a poetic book. When necessary, words will be clarified.

4

The Author and His Trials

The author of Psalm 119 is unknown, as it is not listed in the Psalm. However, most scholars believe that it was David. Another possibility would be Ezra. Personally, I lean toward the notion that David wrote the Psalm, like he did so many others.

One thing we know for sure about the author: he endured many difficulties and trials. An examination of this Psalm reveals much information of a personal nature about the psalmist. Consider the following statements:

- My soul is broken (v 20)
- I am in reproach and contempt (v 22)
- My soul clings to the dust (v 25)
- My soul melts because of heaviness (v 28)
- I dread reproach (v 39)
- I have been in great derision (v 51)
- Indignation has taken hold of me (v 53)
- I suffered affliction when I backslid (v 67)
- My soul faints (v 81)
- My eyes fail (v 82)
- I am like a wineskin in smoke (v 83)
- The proud have dug pits for me (v 85)
- I am persecuted wrongfully (v 86)
- I am almost at my end (v 87)
- The wicked seek to destroy me (v 95)
- I am very much afflicted (v 107)
- My flesh trembles (v 120)

- I am in fear (v 120)
- I shed rivers of tears (v 136)
- I am despised (v 141)
- I am overtaken with trouble and anguish (v 143)
- Consider my affliction (v 153)
- Many are my persecutors (v 157)
- I am disgusted (v 158)
- Princes have persecuted me without cause (v 161)

One thing is for sure: the psalmist kept it real. There was no put-on with him in his prayers to God. But he also kept reminding himself of the truth of God's Word and the keeping power of God. As you go through this prayer devotional for the next 22 days, purpose right now to keep it real with God and don't simply pray *religiously*.

Nine Hebrew Words for the Word of God

Torah

1 Blessed are the undefiled in the way, who walk in the <u>law</u> of the Lord.

The first word we will examine is the Hebrew word *torah* (to-raw'), translated "law" here. Torah is used 219 times in the Old Testament and means, "God's entire instruction to His people." The Jews referred to both the Pentateuch (first five books) and the entire Old Testament as the torah. Interestingly, the word is used in Psalms far more than in any other book (35 times). The second closest count is in Deuteronomy (22 times). The word torah appears in Psalm 119 a total of 25 times.

God attaches His blessing to walking in obedience to His law – His entire instructions. Unfortunately, so many are seeking God's blessing outside of His Word and instructions.

Hosea 4:6 My people are destroyed for lack of knowledge.

During Jeremiah's time, God's leaders became blind and arrogant, using the Word of God for their own profit, much like today.

Jeremiah 2:8 The priests said not, Where is the Lord? and they that handle the law knew me not: the pastors also transgressed against me, and the prophets prophesied by Baal, and walked after things that do not profit.

One word of caution related to the Law is that to embrace it in letter without the Spirit is legalism, producing no blessing. Guard your heart against allowing legalism into your thought process. Allow the Holy Spirit to guide you for God's commandments are not oppressive (1 John 5:3).

`Edah (Eduth)

2 Blessed are they that keep his <u>testimonies</u>, and that seek him with the whole heart.

`Edah (ay-daw), translated "testimonies" here, is used 26 times in the Old Testament and means, "Covenant stipulations or requirements." Sometimes, "testimonies" comes from eduth, which comes from the same root word (59 occurrences). Combined, the words appear 22 times in Psalm 119.

In a covenant, there was the following:

1. Historical Introduction
2. Covenant Stipulations
3. Blessings and Curses

For us here in the twenty-first century, the historical introduction would be the context of the Scriptures and the examples found therein. Of particular interest in our study will be the second part – covenant stipulations. Throughout the Word, there are conditions to be met before the promise is received. As can be seen in verse two, it is not just an outward observance, but a seeking and a following

8

from the whole heart. The blessings and the cursings are the results of the decisions and actions we take. God's desire is to bless us more abundantly than we can imagine.

Derek

---

3 They also do no iniquity: they walk in his <u>ways</u>.

Derek (deh'-rek), translated "ways" here, is used 705 in the Old Testament and means, "God's <u>principles and means of operation</u>." The word appears six times in Psalm 119.

God has a way of operation that He will not violate. We must gain understanding in God's overall objective and His principles for living.

> **Isaiah 55:8-9**
> **8 For my thoughts are not your thoughts, neither are your ways my ways, saith the Lord.**
> **9 For as the heavens are higher than the earth, so are my ways higher than your ways, and my thoughts than your thoughts.**

The Hebrew lexicon goes on in the explanation of this word to say, "a manner and course in life." We must find the course that God has for our lives and walk it out.

Verse 37 says, "Turn away mine eyes from beholding vanity; and quicken thou me in thy way (derek)." Vanity opposes God's ways. A person cannot behold vanity all day and still walk in God's ways. The Bible gives us clear instruction to renew our minds in order to begin thinking God's way.

> **Romans 12:2 And be not conformed to this world: but be ye transformed by the renewing of your mind, that ye may**

prove what is that good, and acceptable, and perfect, will of God.

Piqqud

4 Thou hast commanded us to keep thy <u>precepts</u> diligently.

Piqqud (pik-kood'), translated "precepts" here, is used 24 times in the Old Testament and means, "<u>Detailed instructions from the Lord.</u>" Twenty-one of the 24 usages are found in Psalm 119.

Please note the word *diligently* in this verse when referring to keeping God's precepts. Webster's definition of "diligently" is, "Showing painstaking effort and application in whatever is undertaken." Dedicated effort is required in order to understand God's instructions on a personal level.

The Lord's detailed instructions for our lives require time alone with God, seeking His face. He has a plan – a blueprint with intricate details. He will reveal them on an "as needed" basis when we seek Him with the whole heart. The example of Moses and the building of the tabernacle shows us this.

> **Hebrews 8:5 Who serve unto the example and shadow of heavenly things, as Moses was admonished of God when he was about to make the tabernacle: for, See, saith he, that thou make all things according to the pattern shewed to thee in the mount.**

Moses had to get alone with God on the mount and seek Him before the detailed plans for the tabernacle were revealed.

Regarding God's precepts, we should...

- Meditate on them (v 15)
- Pray to understand them (v 27)
- Hate every false way (v 104)

Choq

5 O that my ways were directed to keep thy <u>statutes</u>!

Choq (khoke), translated "statutes" here, is used 127 times in the Old Testament and means, "God's regulations and boundaries for His people, individually and collectively." The word carries the thought of "cutting into, engraving or inscribing." Choq is used 21 times in Psalm 119.

God cuts into and engraves His boundaries on the tablet of our conscience.

> **Jeremiah 31:33 But this shall be the covenant that I will make with the house of Israel; After those days, saith the Lord, I will put my law in their inward parts, and write it in their hearts; and will be their God, and they shall be my people.**

The psalmist prays to be directed within God's boundaries for his life.

There are three levels of God's boundaries:

1. Universal within creation (e.g., man with a woman – Romans 1)
2. The Statutes of His Word (general)
3. Personal boundaries (these are unique to your call and purpose)

All three levels work in harmony and there is never any contradiction to them.

Mitsvah

> **6 Then shall I not be ashamed, when I have respect unto all thy commandments.**

Mitsvah (mits-vah'), translated "commandments" here, is used 181 times in the Old Testament and means, "God's rules and regulations that express His authority." Mitsvah is found in Psalm 119 a total of 21 times.

The psalmist said that we must respect God's commandments. God gave the 10 Commandments, not the 10 suggestions. Further, looking at God's commands from a New Testament perspective, it must be understood that they are not burdensome.

> **1 John 5:3 For this is the love of God, that we keep His commandments; and His commandments are not grievous.**

God's authority is expressed through the following:

- The divine authority of His Person
- The divine authority of His Word
- His delegated authority within the Church

Additionally, Romans 13 advises us that all authority is established by God, including civil authority. But here in Psalm 119, we are specifically talking about the authority of His Word.

Verse 21 tells us that the proud oppose God's authority (mitsvah). Evildoers will fight against God's commands (v 115). But God's Word will never change and will always win out.

7 I will praise thee with uprightness of heart, when I shall have learned thy righteous judgments.

Mishpat (mish-pawt'), translated "judgments" here, is used 421 times in the Old Testament and means, "God's verdicts as Divine Judge regarding the actions of people with one another." Mishpat is found in Psalm 119 a total of 22 times.

The psalmist emphasizes the importance of praising God and trusting Him in regards to human affairs and dealings with other people. There is a big tie-in between trust and praise.

Romans 12:19 Vengeance is mine; I will repay, saith the Lord.

The child of God must guard his heart from bitterness. Hebrews 12:15 tells us that bitterness will defile a person. This can affect a person spiritually, mentally, emotionally and even physically. It is the commission of all believers to walk in love and forgive all those who trespass against them.

Mishpat also speaks to God's dealings with us as individuals. Hebrews chapter 12 teaches us that God, in His righteous judgments, chastens those whom He loves.

Verse 30 teaches us to lay everything out before God and trust in Him with His judgments. Verse 39 reminds us that God's judgments are good.

9 Wherewithal shall a young man cleanse his way? by taking heed thereto according to thy <u>word</u>.

Dabar (daw-baw'), translated "word" here, is used 1,439 times in the Old Testament and means, "God's revelation in general; His commandments and promises" Dabar is found 23 times in Psalm 119.

The psalmist notes the cleansing power of the Word. The entirety of Scripture speaks to this over and over.

- Our minds need to be renewed to the whole counsel of God's Word. (Romans 12:2)
- Every word of Scripture is God-breathed (2 Timothy 3:16)
- Jesus said that the truth that we know will make us free (John 8:32)

Dabar is used throughout the rest of Psalm 119, including the following verses:

- Verse 11: Hide the *dabar* in your heart
- Verse 38: Be established in God's *dabar*
- Verse 49: Put God in remembrance of His *dabar*

Imrah

11 Thy <u>word</u> have I hid in mine heart, that I might not sin against thee.

Imrah (im-raw'), translated "word" here, is used 37 times in the Old Testament and means, "God's spoken word." Imrah is mentioned a total of 16 times in Psalm 119.

This word is similar to the New Testament Greek word, *rhema* – the spoken word of God. An imrah (or a rhema) happens when we get intimate with God through His Word. A person can choose to study the Word of God entirely on an academic level and learn many things. But only when we allow God to speak into our hearts through His Word will we experience the spoken word of God, through the witness and confirmation of the Holy Spirit.

Day 1

Aleph

1 Blessed are the undefiled in the way, who walk in the law [torah] of the Lord [Yahweh].

What a beautiful way to start the Psalm – by speaking of how to be blessed. Blessing from God comes from being undefiled in our daily living and walking out the principles of God's entire Word (Heb. Torah) – all of His instruction. God does not truly bless us apart from living by His Word. As Christians, we must learn how to put into practice the daily application of God's Word – the entirety of His instruction.

Lord, I desire Your blessing on my life. Remove from me the defilement of the world and its ways. Help me to walk in the entirety of Your Word and all of Your instruction for my life.

---

2 Blessed are they that keep his testimonies [edah], and that seek him with the whole heart.

Again with God's blessing. The Lord wants to bless us more than we want to be blessed. *Testimonies* means, "Covenant stipulations or requirements." The covenant promises of God require our obedience. God knows when we are seeking Him shallowly for what we *want* or when we are seeking Him with our whole heart because we love Him. Half-heartedness will never be satisfied with the fullness of God's presence. Only when we seek Him with our whole hearts will He be found by us (Jeremiah 29:13).

Father, help me to be a doer of your Word and a keeper of Your testimonies. Thank you that I am in covenant with You through the blood of Jesus. Help me to put away half-heartedness and to seek You with my whole heart.

---

3 They also do no iniquity: they walk in his ways [derek].

Those who are followers of Christ do not practice a lifestyle of sin. Sinless perfection was only ever accomplished by one Man – our Lord and Savior. But as we walk with the Lord and obey the light that He gives, He continuously cleanses us from all sin (1 John 1:7-9). The word *derek* is referring to God's principles or His way of doing things. As we follow Jesus and develop our relationship with Him, we increase our understanding of His ways.

Jesus, thank You for saving me and setting me free from the bondage of sin. Take me into greater levels of freedom in You. Help me to walk in Your ways and cast aside every sin and weight that would hold me back.

---

4 Thou hast commanded us to keep thy precepts [piqqud] diligently.

"Precepts" is the word *piqqud* and means, "Detailed instructions from the Lord." Spend some time praying that God would reveal the details of His plan for your life. This will require diligence and persistence, but the Lord will be faithful to answer (Jeremiah 33:3). Synonyms of *diligence* include *attentiveness* and *persistence*. Many will say they want God's will, but are you so sincere about your desire that you are willing to invest time and effort seeking Him and His Word?

Oh Lord, I want to know the detailed instructions that You have for my life. Help me to seek You with my whole heart in order to find You and know You in a greater way.

5 O that my ways were directed to keep thy statutes [choq]!

"Statutes" is the word *khoke* and means, "God's regulations and boundaries for His people, individually and collectively." God wants us to remain within the boundaries He establishes for our lives – not as a punishment but as protection. God's Spirit within us is how we are able to live out God's Word. Otherwise, we are just trying to comply with a list of rules that never produce life.

Father, thank You for the boundaries You establish in my life. I ask that You would direct my ways to stay within them. Bring me back in when I sway outside the lines.

6 Then shall I not be ashamed, when I have respect unto all thy commandments [mitsvah].

"Commandments" is the word *mitsvah* and means, "God's rules and regulations that express His authority." At one point, Jesus told His followers, "Why do you call me 'Lord, Lord,' and not do what I tell you?" (Luke 6:46). When we follow God's commandments, we will never be ashamed before the Lord.

Lord, I give You respect in my life. You have complete authority to do in me and in my life, all that You desire. I submit myself to Your rule.

7 I will praise thee with uprightness of heart, when I shall have learned thy righteous judgments [mishpat].

Praise is more than singing songs at church. Praise is a lifestyle for the believer. David was foremost known as a worshipper. It's easy to praise God when all is going favorably, but it's important to praise God in the difficult seasons of life. I have learned that *the praise the costs the most, counts the most.*   This is especially true when we feel that we have been wronged by another. The Hebrew word for *judgments* is *mishpat* and means, "God's verdicts as Divine Judge regarding the actions of people with one another." Instead of defending yourself against false accusations, try praising God with uprightness of heart.

Lord, I offer praise to You – no matter what it looks like, no matter what I feel like. You are in control and I choose to allow You to fight my battles. Help me to keep my heart upright and to prevent taking up an offense.

_____

_____

_____

8 I will keep thy statutes [choq]: O forsake me not utterly.

God watches over His Word to perform it (Jeremiah 1:12). As we keep His Word, God is always actively working in our life and situation. Hebrews 13:5 tells us that Jesus will never leave us or forsake us. The original word for *leave* in that verse means to, "loosen the grip." Not only is Jesus never going to walk away from you, but He will never even loosen His grip!

Thank You Jesus that You are always with me. Help me to keep Your statutes and stay within Your boundaries. I don't want to be a hearer of Your Word only; make me a doer of Your Word, O Lord.

Day 2

Beth

9 Wherewithal shall a young man cleanse his way? by taking heed thereto according to thy word [dabar].

There is a cleansing that comes from God's Word that is like no other. The word translated *cleanse* (*zakah*) means "to make pure." Many Christians try to walk with God and be strong in their faith without the benefit of a clear conscience. But you can never have full confidence without being cleansed. Jesus said, "Now you are clean through the word which I have spoken to you" (John 15:3). True freedom comes from knowing the Word of God (John 8:32).

Lord, cleanse me today with Your Word. Purge from me all of the dross and impurity that keeps me from being all that You want me to be. I purpose my heart to give careful attention to Your Word in my life.

_____

_____

_____

10 With my whole heart have I sought thee: O let me not wander from thy commandments [mitsvah].

True believers *seek* while pretend believers *sneak*. God promised that He would be found by anyone who seeks for Him with his or her whole heart (Jeremiah 29:13). Wandering from God's commandments happens a little at a time. Compromise creeps up on us until it has a foothold. It isn't where you start, but rather if you finish that counts. Guard your heart from wandering.

'O God, I seek You with my whole heart. I empty myself before You and ask that You would fill me up with Your love. Keep me from wandering from Your great commandments Lord. Help me to guard my heart from compromise dear Jesus.

_____

_____

_____

11 Thy word [imrah] have I hid in mine heart, that I might not sin against thee.

Hiding God's Word in your heart is a process of diligence. It is a daily exercise of reading and meditating on the Scriptures until they become engrafted or implanted into your soul. As a practice, I have never set out to memorize Scripture verses, yet I can quote hundreds. The closer we get to God and the more we abide in the Word and allow it to abide in us, the less we want to sin against our Lord. The word used here for *word* is *imrah* and means "spoken word." It is similar to the New Testament Greek word, rhema – the spoken word of God.

Help me Lord to hide Your Word in my heart that I might live a life that is pleasing to You. Deliver me from every hidden attitude that conflicts with Your grace and empower me through Your Word and Spirit to live a holy life unto You.

---

12 Blessed art thou, O Lord [Yahweh]: teach me thy statutes [choq].

The psalmist shows his adoration for God here. "Blessed are You, O Yahweh!" Yahweh is the covenant name of God. We may bless Him because we are in covenant relationship with Him. The plea is then entered for Yahweh to teach him His statutes. Understanding of God's Word will flow from a place of adoration of God. Remember the two disciples on the road to Emmaus after the resurrection? Although, they didn't know it was Jesus at the time, their hearts burned within them as He spoke the truth of the Word (Luke 24:13-35).

O Lord, Yahweh, Mighty God, I love You so much. Bless Your holy name. I pray that You would teach me Your statutes.

---

13 With my lips have I declared all the judgments [mishpat] of thy mouth.

In other words, teach me and I will teach others, Lord. Jesus said, "Man shall not live by bread alone, but by every word that proceeds from the mouth of God" (Matthew 4:4). God's verdicts for living are clearly laid out in His Word. As followers of Christ we must know that taking up our cross and following Him means the forfeiture of our personal rights and opinions. It's so easy for people to speak what's on their mind. But does our opinion line up with God's judgments?

Open doors for me today God. Give me opportunities to share Your Word and Your love with those who need it the most. Season me with Your grace so that I may speak the truth in love. Help me to check my opinions and attitudes for Your glory.

---

14 I have rejoiced in the way of thy testimonies [eduth], as much as in all riches.

Jesus told us that we couldn't serve both God and mammon/money (Matthew 6:24). God's Word is greater in every way than all riches. His Word will sustain us in the worst of times. All of the promises of God are 'yes and amen' (2 Corinthians 1:20). The wonderful thing about serving God is that if you place Him first in your life, He will supply your every need. It all comes down to priorities.

Lord, I rejoice in the way of Your testimonies. You bring truth into my life at just the right time and in the way that I need it. I cling to Your promises for my life. My trust is not in uncertain riches, but in Your Word, O God, that abides forever.

---

15 I will meditate in thy precepts [piqqud], and have respect unto thy ways.

Meditating in God's Word is a biblical key to success (Joshua 1:8). It has been discovered that the average person thinks about 50,000 thoughts a day and that 95% of them are the same every day. If we can harness our thoughts to meditate on God's Word, our lives will be so much stronger for the Lord. As we meditate on God's Word, our minds are renewed (Romans 12:2). This is a transformational process that brings us fully into alignment with God's will.

Help me Lord to use Your Word as my meditation throughout my day. With Your help, I cast down every argument in my thought life and take every thought captive to Your obedience. I respect all of Your ways God. Help me to line my life up to Your Word.

_____

_____

_____

16 I will delight myself in thy statutes [chuqqah]: I will not forget thy word [dabar].

Being forgetful of God's Word is a big problem in the lives of Christians. If we will delight ourselves daily in God's Word then the Holy Spirit will bring it to our remembrance when we need it. The NIV translation uses the word *neglect* instead of *forget*. This is really the main problem – neglecting the Word. Choose today to begin delighting in the Word and making time to study and meditate on it.

Lord, I delight myself in Your Word – all of Your Word, all of the time. Take me into deeper places in the knowledge of the truth. Bring Your Word to my remembrance when I need it the most, Lord.

_____

_____

_____

Day 3

Gimel

17 Deal bountifully with thy servant, that I may live, and keep thy word [dabar].

Without the bountiful grace of God we can do nothing to positively affect the world in which we live. In Him we live and move and have our being (Acts 17:28). The only hope that we have of keeping His Word is through the power of the Holy Spirit within us. Interestingly, the Hebrew word for "deal bountifully" (*gamal*) means "to wean." As I ponder the meaning of God weaning me, I realize that God must wean me from trusting in my own resources in order to bountifully supply my needs.

Thank You Father for Your bountiful grace and mercy in my life. I utterly depend upon You in every way. I want to live my in obedience to Your Word.

_____

_____

_____

18 Open thou mine eyes, that I may behold wondrous things out of thy law [torah].

Intellectual knowledge of the Word may be helpful in some ways – from an academic standpoint. But it still will not produce life – the anointing. Only spiritual knowledge of the Word will produce life. The Holy Spirit is the only one who can produce this life-giving, fruit-producing knowledge within us. This cannot happen apart from relationship with Jesus. It is my prayer that as you meditate and pray through Psalm 119, using this devotional, that God will open your eyes to a greater understanding of His Word.

O Lord, open my eyes; grant me revelation of Your Word. So many wondrous things in Your Word and I want to know them all Lord. Cause revelation to be released in my heart as I pray through this Psalm.

---

19 I am a stranger in the earth: hide not thy commandments [mitsvah] from me.

Too often we find ourselves getting attached to our surroundings. We must always remember that we are sojourners. Our citizenship is in heaven (Philippians 3:20). I always think of myself as a square peg in a round hole here on earth. We were made for so much more than this earthly abode. Eternity awaits. Because we are just passing through, we need His Word so much more in our lives as a compass to direct and a comfort in our affliction.

Lord, keep me hidden Your presence. I am in this world, but I do not belong to it. I belong to You Jesus. Keep nothing back from me. Don't hide Your precious Word from my understanding. Thank You for keeping me until the last day.

---

20 My soul breaketh for the longing that it hath unto thy judgments [mishpat] at all times.

How much do you hunger and thirst for God's Word? Does it ever feel as if your *soul is breaking*? The NLT renders this, "I am always overwhelmed with a desire..." This is such a beautiful passion that's shown here by the psalmist. God will always feed us to the level of our hunger – never more. The Bible is clear that if we will draw near to God that He will draw near to us (James 4:8). Today, ask God to birth in you a greater desire and longing for His Word.

Father, my soul is overwhelmed with a hunger for Your Word. Fill me up Lord! Produce in me a greater hunger for all that You have for my life.

---

21 Thou hast rebuked the proud that are cursed, which do err from thy commandments [mitsvah].

Pride is God repellant. God resists the proud but gives grace to the humble (James 4:6). One who is filled with pride will go astray from the commandments of God. Remember, commandments are "God's rules and regulations that express His authority." The prideful refuse to submit to God's authority. Jesus once asked, "Why do you call me, 'Lord, Lord,' and do not do what I say?" (Luke 6:46).

Lord, I humble myself before You and ask You to strip me from all fleshly pride. Help me to stay humble before You and never stray from Your commandments.

22 Remove from me reproach and contempt; for I have kept thy testimonies [edah].

David endured a life filled with reproach in his early days. Scorn, contempt and taunting were leveled at him, including by his own brothers. His own father did not consider him important enough to be brought before Samuel for consideration as king, as were his brothers. Through it all, even with King Saul trying to kill him multiple times, David kept his heart pure before God and kept His testimonies. This was a period in David's life that taught him the valuable lesson of humility, which served him well throughout his lifetime. Though the flesh feels weakened by the persecution, if we keep our hearts pure before God, He will ultimately use it for our good and His glory.

Father, You are my source. My identity is in You. Though others may persecute me for it, I will keep Your testimonies. Strengthen me when I am weak and help me to trust You as my defense. Remove me from their thoughts and evil intentions.

23 Princes also did sit and speak against me: but thy servant did meditate in thy statutes [choq].

The powers of the world stood in opposition to David because He trusted in the one true God – Yahweh. *Sitting* denotes continuance, meaning that the persecution was persistent. Through it all, David was not discouraged from meditating in God's Word and standing strong in his convictions. It has been said that a person's character is never truly revealed until it is fully tested. In the economy of God this is ever so true. The New Testament Greek word for *economy* (*oikonomia*) means "household management." God has a way of doing things in His household and His people are His utmost concern. In order for God to take you where you need to go, there will be naysayers as part of the process. Keep the Word of God as the meditation of your heart.

Lord, though the world may speak against me, I know that they hated You first. By Your help, I refuse to withdrawal from my convictions in Your Word. I will meditate in Your Word O God as my source of strength and courage.

_____

_____

_____

24 Thy testimonies [edah] also are my delight and my counselors.

Man-made rules are burdensome and tedious, but God's testimonies should be a delight for the Christian. As we follow His testimonies, God will protect and bless us. We are wise when we allow His testimonies to be our counselor. Steer clear of people who give advice that opposes what the Bible teaches. In the multitude of godly counselors, there is safety (Proverbs 11:14). In my role as pastor, I frequently get folks wanting me to make their decisions for them. "What should I do, pastor?" My position in that scenario is to counsel them with the Word of God and never make their decision for them. Each of us need to have a strong conviction on what the Word says and how it applies.

O Lord, You are my delight. Through Your testimonies I draw closer to You. Even though I may not always understand, I trust and delight in Your instruction for my life. Surround me with godly counselors who will speak Your testimonies into my life.

_____

_____

_____

Day 4

Daleth

25 My soul cleaveth unto the dust: quicken thou me according to thy word [dabar].

Here we see the desperate condition of the psalmist. Likely in a fiery trial, he pours out his soul before the Lord. The word *quicken* means to "make alive." Though he is in a spiritually dry place, he knows that God has not abandoned him and he requests that the Lord would bring life into his soul. How often do we feel much the same during the struggles of life? If we ask, God will breathe life into our souls.

Dear Lord, here I am again asking for You to revive me. The enemy has taken his shots at me and I feel lifeless in spirit, but I know You are with me. I pray O God that You would fill me with Your life and raise me up for Your Glory. With nothing else to stand upon, I rest on Your Word.

_____

_____

_____

26 I have declared my ways, and thou heardest me: teach me thy statutes [choq].

The word *declare* means "to recount." The psalmist laid out all his ways before the Lord in prayer. There are times when we just need to empty our hearts before a compassionate Father who hears us. There is great comfort in knowing that the Lord hears us. He hears us in a way that no one else can. While we wish others could read our minds at times, the Lord really can. He fully understands us and yet loves us without condition.

Lord, You know me like on one else. Even though you know my needs, You tell me to ask. Thank You for hearing me and being attentive to my needs and problems. Teach me Your statutes Lord. Give me a teachable heart and an open mind. I am hungry for Your truth in my life.

---

27 Make me to understand the way of thy precepts [piqqud]: so shall I talk of thy wondrous works.

The word for *precepts* (*piqqud*) means "detailed instructions from the Lord." God so very much wants us to understand the detailed instructions that He has for our lives. Jesus taught us to pray, "Your kingdom come; Your will be done on earth as it is in heaven" (Matthew 6:10). There is a key to discovering these heavenly details: seek Him with the whole heart (Jeremiah 29:13; 33:3). When we understand His perfect plan for our lives and begin to walk in it, we cannot but speak of His wonderful works!

Father, I yield my life to You and seek You with my whole heart. Reveal to my heart Your perfect will – the detailed instructions for my

life that You ordained before the foundations of the world. Grant
unto me the boldness to speak of You and Your wondrous works.

_____

_____

_____

28 My soul melteth for heaviness: strengthen thou me according unto thy word [dabar].

The Hebrew word for *melteth* (*dalaph*) means "to weep." God remembers that we are but dust (Psalm 103:14). The test and trials of this life can break our soul – but not beyond His repair. The word for *heaviness* (*tugah*) means "grief, depression, sorrow." Depression can be a real problem in the lives of God's people, but we must keep coming back to the center – trust in God. He will strengthen us in our weaknesses and uphold us with His love.

Father, You know my struggles and my sorrows. I lean on You in my
adversity. I ask that You would strengthen me according to Your
Word. Heal my heart and renew the joy of my salvation.

_____

_____

_____

29 Remove from me the way of lying: and grant me thy law [torah] graciously.

There is so much deceit in this world. The Christian must guard his heart and keep on the belt of truth. Truthfulness is a lifestyle and is absolutely essential to an overcoming life. It's easy to begin believing the lies of the enemy if we are not filling ourselves up with the Word of God. Thus, the psalmist prays: "Grant me Thy law graciously."

Lord, for so long I believed the lies of the devil about myself. But Your Word has revealed the truth that You love me. Remove out of my life every deceitful tactic of the enemy and fill me up with the Word of God.

---

30 I have chosen the way of truth: thy judgments [mishpat] have I laid before me.

God makes plain throughout Scripture the importance of choices. We are to choose whom we will serve (Joshua 24:15). We are to choose between life and death, blessing and cursing (Deuteronomy 30:19). We must also choose to believe God's Word for ourselves. The psalmist laid out all of God's judgments before him and concluded that in every instance, God was faithful. Choose today to believe God's Word.

Father, You watch over Your Word to perform it. It is impossible for You to lie. Today, I choose the way of truth instead of my own way. You will lead me into blessing as I follow You.

---

31 I have stuck unto thy testimonies [eduth]: O Lord [Yahweh], put me not to shame.

There are going to be times when you are tested. Circumstances will try to pull you away from your faith in God and His Word. In those times, stick to God's Word even closer. The Lord will never let you be put to shame when you trust in Him.

Lord, help me to stick to Your testimonies in times of trouble. No matter what it looks like, I know that You are in control. You will confirm Your Word in my life and cause me to never be put to shame.

---

32 I will run the way of thy commandments [mitsvah], when thou shalt enlarge my heart.

There is an important principle being shared here. When we allow God to enlarge our heart to desire more of Him, we will more readily run the way of His commandments. Some things we are not ready to hear from the Lord, early in our relationship. But as we become more seasoned in the Spirit, more revelation knowledge is granted. To whom much is given, much is required.

Lord, enlarge my heart. Increase my capacity to learn and hear from You. I will run the way of Your commandments O God as You give me revelation knowledge of Your Word.

Day 5

He

33 Teach me, O Lord [Yahweh], the way of thy statutes [choq]; and I shall keep it unto the end.

The purpose for learning the Word of God is to put it into practice in daily living and to draw closer to God. God does not teach us in order to puff us up with head knowledge. Sadly, there are many who know *about* God through the diligence of study, but don't allow the Holy Spirit to bring them into an intimate knowledge of the Lord.

Teach me, O Lord, the way of Your statutes. I want to be a doer of the Word all the days of my life. I don't want to just know about You, Lord, but to intimately know You.

---

34 Give me understanding, and I shall keep thy law [torah]; yea, I shall observe it with my whole heart.

Understanding is a precious commodity. True understanding comes from God, through relationship with Him and study of His living Word. We cannot keep a law that we cannot understand. Further, many try to keep the letter of the law instead of the spirit. The Bible tells us "the letter kills, but the spirit gives life" (2 Corinthians 3:6). God wants us to observe (i.e., practice) His Word with our whole heart.

Lord God, grant me spiritual understanding of Your Word. I want to see the hidden treasures in Your Word. I pray that the Holy Spirit would be my instructor, taking me into deeper places of understanding. Help me to hold nothing back from You Lord, but to seek You with my whole heart.

---

35 Make me to go in the path of thy commandments [mitsvah]; for therein do I delight.

It takes more than human volition to go in the path of God's commandments. It requires the life of the Spirit of God within us to walk this way. Many have had good intentions, but without the enabling power of the Spirit, the human will is futile in its attempts to walk in God's will. This requires surrender to God and therein is there true delight.

Father, may Your will be done in my life, just as it is in heaven. I desire to walk in the path of Your commandments and to please You. Fill me up, Lord. Use me up, Lord. I delight in You and all Your ways.

36 Incline my heart unto thy testimonies [eduth], and not to covetousness.

The word *incline* means "to predispose." Before we come to Christ, we have all sorts of predispositions from the fallen nature. Now that we belong to Him, our predispositions are toward His testimonies. Covetousness is the old nature and must be put under.

Lord, I ask that my heart would continually be inclined unto Your testimonies. Help me to walk by the new nature You have given me. I put aside the covetousness of the old nature and walk in newness of life by Your Spirit.

37 Turn away mine eyes from beholding vanity; and quicken thou me in thy way [derek].

There is so much vanity in the world. The word means "emptiness deceitfulness, worthlessness and nothingness." Yet somehow, Satan dresses it up so beautifully in order to ensnare the hearts of people. When we behold – fix our attention to, things that are worthless and void of good it robs us of our focus on God's will. If a person's whole life is centered on social media, television, music, et al, then there is very little room for God's Word to guide one's life.

Dear Lord, deliver me from vanity – nothingness that Satan dresses up to appear as something. Help me to turn my eyes away from it today by instead fixing my gaze upon Your Word and Your way. Revive me O God to do Your will for my life.

38 Stablish thy word [imrah] unto thy servant, who is devoted to thy fear.

The Bible speaks much about being established – rooted and grounded. The only way this happens is through God's Word. Before we can bear fruit that remains, we must allow the root of God's Word go deep within us. This will prevent the storms of life from easily uprooting us from God's vineyard. To be devoted to God's fear is to live our lives in reverential awe of a Holy God.

O God, I pray that You would establish me in Your Word. As I study it and meditate upon it, cause the roots to go deeper and deeper. Without You, I can do nothing Lord. I devote myself to walking holy before You.

---

39 Turn away my reproach which I fear: for thy judgments [mishpat] are good.

Reproach is the persecution that comes by being a follower of Christ. The world will hate you because it first hated Him (John 15:18). This is not to say that we shouldn't ask God to turn it away from us, as the psalmist does. David acknowledged that God's judgments are good.

Lord, I know that persecution will come. It happens because I follow You. But I ask You to protect me from the harm that the reproach and slander can cause. Be my defense O Lord. All of Your judgments are good and I trust in You alone as my refuge.

---

40 Behold, I have longed after thy precepts [piqqud]: quicken me in thy righteousness.

As people, we *long after* or desire many things throughout life. But there is so much vanity in much of what we desire. As God purifies our heart and draws us closer to Him, our desires begin to change. The more of the Word that you put into your life, the greater the hunger there is for more. In this intimacy, the detailed instructions from the Lord for our life begin to unfold. God makes us alive and revives us in His righteousness.

Father, I thirst for Your Word. Fill me up with Your precepts – Your detailed instructions for my life. There are times when I am complacent and I need revived. Make me alive in Your righteousness, O God.

Day 6

Waw

41 Let thy mercies come also unto me, O Lord [Yahweh], even thy salvation, according to thy word [imrah].

God's mercies are new every morning (Lamentations 3:23). There is no one who stands outside of the need of God's mercy. Self-righteousness is a stench in the nostrils of God. Salvation is according to God's Word. The Bible reveals that all of man's good works are not sufficient to be saved (Ephesians 2:8-9). Biblical salvation is found solely in the cross. Salvation is 100% the grace of God; it is not 75/25 or even 99/1.

O Lord, I ask for Your mercy this day in my life. Over and over again I come short of Your glory. I need Your lovingkindness and tender mercy heavenly Father. Thank You for my salvation. I rest in the promise of Your Word that You will also keep me unto the final day.

_____

_____

_____

42 So shall I have wherewith to answer him that reproacheth me: for I trust in thy word [dabar].

When we are verbally attacked the first thing we want to do is fire back in the flesh. A wise person will refrain from this course. If we are to respond (and sometimes it is wiser not to), the Holy Spirit will give us the words to speak at the proper time. As You trust in the Word, God will defend you. "When a man's ways please the Lord, He makes even his enemies to be at peace with him" (Proverbs 16:7).

God, You are my defender. You fill my mouth with what I need to say, if I need to say anything. I trust in You and I trust in Your Word, O Lord. Grant me wisdom to know when to speak and when to hold my tongue.

---

43 And take not the word [dabar] of truth utterly out of my mouth; for I have hoped in thy judgments [mishpat].

In other words, "Lord, let the evidence of Your blessing be on my life as I speak Your Word." Romans 1:16 tells us to not be ashamed of the gospel of Jesus Christ for it is the power of God unto salvation. The original word for *ashamed* means "to disappoint, to fail to show up." When we are not ashamed of Him, He will always show up and will never abandon us. Our hope is in Him.

Lord, You have my full surrender. I choose to talk the talk and also walk the walk. I know that You will never abandon or disappoint me, Lord. I have a cheerful, confident expectancy that You will cause Your blessing to remain on my life.

---

44 So shall I keep thy law [torah] continually for ever and ever.

At all times and at all places, O Lord, I will keep Your Word! Being a doer of the Word of God is about more than doing so when it is convenient, or advantageous for me. It's a life-long commitment to the Word that impacts every area of our life.

O God, help me to practice Your Word in all seasons of my life. Even when I don't see or feel Your hand working, I will move forward by faith. Thank You for giving me an eternal perspective and an understanding that it's not all about me. Use me for Your glory and to fulfill Your purpose for my life.

45 And I will walk at liberty: for I seek thy precepts [piqqud].

This verse makes me want to shout! It's one thing to talk about liberty, but quite another to walk at liberty. The term *walk* is used throughout the Bible as a metaphor for daily living. It's great to feel liberty when we are at church, but even better when we translate that victory to our daily living. This can be done by learning and practicing God's Word – His instructions for daily living.

Father, thank You that all that the Lord sets free are free indeed. Through Your Word I am learning to walk at liberty in my daily life. Help me to walk in the light as You are in the light and may the power of the blood cleanse me from all sin and free me from all bondage.

46 I will speak of thy testimonies [edah] also before kings, and will not be ashamed.

We never really know how the Lord is going to use us until we fully live a life of obedience to Him. Proverbs tells us, "A man's gift makes room for him, and brings him before great men" (18:16). If we are not ashamed, the Lord will use us in magnificent ways. God is the one who opens the doors and He qualifies the called, instead of calling the qualified. Get ready and ask the Lord to use you.

Lord, I ask for divine favor to speak about You before all that You send me, including kings and those in authority. Cause Your face to shine upon me and anoint me to speak for You. Help me to never be ashamed of You and to always speak the truth in love.

47 And I will delight myself in thy commandments [mitsvah], which I have loved.

What does it mean to actively delight yourself in God's Word? The word *delight* means to take great pleasure and satisfaction from something. Jesus told us that the heaven (atmosphere) and the earth would pass away, but God's Word would remain forever (Matthew 24:35). I have discovered that the more time I spend in God's Word, the greater delight I have in my studies. When you allow your time in the Word to get squeezed out by other stuff, the delight begins to wane. Pray today for God to reignite your heart with a desire for His Word.

O Lord, fill my heart up with a desire for Your Word. I want to delight in Your commandments. Everything around me will ultimately fade, but Your Word remains forever. Reignite my heart to hunger for Your Word.

---

48 My hands also will I lift up unto thy commandments [mitsvah], which I have loved; and I will meditate in thy statutes [choq].

Lifting hands in worship is a Biblical practice. For so many years, most traditional churches frowned upon for some reason. But it seems that with the rise of contemporary worship music that it has become a more accepted practice in all Christian churches. This is a good trend. Lifting hands is an outward expression of one's heart surrender to God.

Lord Jesus, I lift my hands in worship to You. I fix my gaze upon You O Lord. I love Your Word and I will meditate in Your statutes day and night.

Day 7

Zayin

49 Remember the word [dabar] unto thy servant, upon which thou hast caused me to hope.

It's an interesting study to look at all the times in the Bible when man is asking God to remember things. Conversely, God asks man to remember, numerous times. The word *remember* is in the Bible 230 times. God remembers His Word because He watches over it to perform it (Jeremiah 1:12). As a follower of Christ, a person should know many of God's wonderful promises that are for His children. God's promises always bring great hope into the heart. Some don't realize how important hope is, but without hope, faith has no target. "Faith is the substance of things *hoped for*" (Hebrews 11:1).

O God, I put You in remembrance of Your promises found in Your Word. All of them are 'yes and amen' in Christ. I trust in Your provision; I trust in Your healing; I trust You in all my ways dear Lord. Watch over Your Word to perform it in my life.

50 This is my comfort in my affliction: for thy word [imrah] hath quickened me.

This temporary world comes with trials and afflictions. Jesus told us to be of good cheer because He has overcome the world (John 16:33). As overcomers, we need the constant supply of God's Word to revive us. When I find myself in troubled situations, the presence of God's peace is enough comfort for me to know that God is working and I just need to trust Him in the situation.

Thank You Lord that You are my comfort. Your Word is my source of instruction for every problem. I need to have greater trust in You, O Lord. I pray that You would revive me with Your Word. Give me a word in season in order to overcome my weariness.

---

51 The proud have had me greatly in derision: yet have I not declined from thy law [torah].

The proud are always the enemy of God's work. Pride is God-repellent, as God resists them (James 4:6). The proud never think twice about coming against God's anointed. They take pleasure is slandering God's leaders. David declared that in all of the persecution he did not decline or turn away from God's Word. When your enemies come against you the fiercest, cling tightly to the Word of God.

O Lord, the proud have rejected You and Your counsel. They slander and lie in order to discredit Your servant and Your work. Deal with them according to Your will. I humble myself in Your presence O Lord. You will protect me and raise me up.

52 I remembered thy judgments [mishpat] of old, O Lord [Yahweh]; and have comforted myself.

Once more we see the reference to *remembering*. This time, however, it is the psalmist remembering God's work in past times. There is great comfort in remembering God's faithfulness in times past. When you dwell on the problems of the present moment it's easy to lose sight of God's goodness throughout your lifetime. Sit down and intentionally start calling to remembrance the answered prayers in your history with God. Israel always made the mistake of forgetting all that God had done for them.

Lord, I remember Your faithfulness to me throughout my lifetime. Even during the hardest of times You brought me through. Comfort me Lord with Your Word. Thank You for Your unfailing love.

53 Horror hath taken hold upon me because of the wicked that forsake thy law [torah].

How easy is it to block out the evil that is so prevalent in our world today? Oh it's not hard to be aware of it, but it can become easy to become numb to it and block it out. After all, if it doesn't personally affect us, why not just live and let live? The psalmist, thankfully, didn't see things that way. The Hebrew word for "horror" (*zalaphah*) is only found three times in the Bible and means "a burning indignation." The things that offend God should offend God's people. Many churches and denominations have even forsaken God's law and are part of the throng that calls evil good and good evil (Isaiah 5:20).

Father, break my heart with what breaks Yours. People all around me forsake Your law O God. I pray for their hearts to be convicted and drawn to Jesus. Forgive the sin, heal the land and bring revival.

---

54 Thy statutes [choq] have been my songs in the house of my pilgrimage.

Learning and meditating on God's Word through song is a great way to grow in the Lord. Lyrical content is so important when it comes to Christian music. Always take time to look at the lyrics to see if they are strong in Biblical content. God often uses songs in a prophetic way when we are going through adversity during our pilgrimage here on earth. For example, you may be drawn to a song that you listen to over and over during a difficult season. It speaks to you and uplifts you. When the same is season is over, it's still a good song, but it no longer has the same impact.

Lord, thank You for the many songs the lift up and glorify Your name. Speak to me through these songs and also Your amazing Psalms in the Word. I remember that I am just passing through here and that this is not my home. Come quickly Lord Jesus.

---

55 I have remembered thy name, O Lord [Yahweh], in the night, and have kept thy law [torah].

So many people have difficulty sleeping at night. One of the main reasons is the mind won't "shut down." It continues to race with thought and worries – mostly about things we can't control. How wonderful it is, instead, to remember and think upon the Lord's name and rest in His peace. Cast all your cares upon the Lord (1 Peter 5:7) trust Him (Proverbs 3:5-6).

God, my trust is in You and Your name is my meditation day and night. There are so many things I can't control, but I choose not to worry about them. You will make all my crooked paths straight. I will practice all of Your Word – the entirety of Your instruction.

---

56 This I had, because I kept thy precepts [piqqud].

This I had, or *this has become mine...* (NASB). All of this – God's Word, needs to become *yours*. It must become personal knowledge through the Holy Spirit who lives in you as a believer. Remember, the word *piqqud* means detailed instructions from the Lord. God's Word is of a personal nature and within it are the details needed for a successful life of following Christ.

Holy Spirit, I thank You that You are making the Word of God personal to me. I apply it into my life on a daily basis. Open my eyes to revelation knowledge. I so very much want Your detailed instructions for my life.

Day 8

Heth

57 Thou art my portion, O Lord [Yahweh]: I have said that I would keep thy words [dabar].

Four times in the Psalms, the Lord is referred to as the psalmist's *portion*. For the Lord to be our portion means to be our *inheritance*. Others may relish in material things or status, but not those who've been captivated by His love. Our portion is the Lord. We keep His Word, not from obligation or duty, but from love and devotion.

No one but You, O Lord, could ever be my portion. You alone satisfy the longing in my soul. Your love is unfailing and never ending. Help me to keep Your Word out of a pure heart of devotion.

_____

_____

_____

58 I intreated thy favour with my whole heart: be merciful unto me according to thy word [imrah].

Favor in the Hebrew (*panim*) means *face*. To seek God's face is to know His favor. It might seem that to experience God's favor and blessing that one needs to seek God's hand – His power and will to act. However, when you seek the Lord with no ulterior agenda, but to just know Him, it will cause His favor and blessing to shine upon you.

Lord, with my whole heart I seek You. Be merciful to me according to Your spoken Word. Sustain me today with Your lovingkindness.

---

59 I thought on my ways, and turned my feet unto thy testimonies [eduh].

There is a way that seems right to the finite mind of man, but the end result is always failure and death (Proverbs 16:25). Much like the prodigal who came to his senses (Luke 15:17), to think on one's ways and then turn to God is the beautiful path to grace. God's ways are higher than our ways and His thoughts than our thoughts (Isaiah 55:8-9).

Lord, today I choose to trust You and forfeit my own way of doing things. I set my mind and my feet into alignment with Your testimonies.

---

60 I made haste, and delayed not to keep thy commandments [mitsvah].

When the psalmist thought on his ways (v 59), he made haste to keep God's commands. The Hebrew word for haste (*chuwsh*) means "to be eager with excitement." It is one thing to keep God's commands out of obligation, but another to do so with eager excitement. This is what Isaiah is getting at when he says, "The willing and obedient will eat the good of the land" (Isaiah 1:19).

God, I run to You with a humble heart. I have made so many excuses in the past and delayed the keeping of Your commands. No more excuses from me about why I can't do it Your way. I surrender Lord.

---

61 The bands of the wicked have robbed me: but I have not forgotten thy law [torah].

Why? This is the nagging echo that haunts so many believers. Why did God allow evil to strike an arrow in me? Why is there suffering and pain to so many good and godly people? The bands of the wicked will continue in this world until such time that all things are put under the feet of Jesus (Hebrews 2:8). Satan is the god of this world and continues to blind the minds of those who don't believe (2 Corinthians 4:4). One day evil will be no more. Until then, we contend and overcome in Christ. In the midst of evil, as followers of Christ, we must persevere and not forget God's law. Many denominations, instead, have watered down the Word of God and become just like the world in their views. But we must uphold God's standard, even as evil continues to worsen.

Thank You Father that I have victory in Jesus. The bands of the wicked can steal my coat but they cannot steal my dream! I will not forget Your law. Your Word is as relevant today as it ever was and I will continue to live by it and proclaim it even if it's unpopular.

62 At midnight I will rise to give thanks unto thee because of thy righteous judgments [mishpat].

The psalmist was kept wakeful by his constant meditation of God's Word. I listen to the Word of God via my mobile device as I go to sleep each night and through the night. There are many times when I am so captivated in my listening that I stay awake. The Bible says to "Give thanks in every situation" (1 Thessalonians 5:18). Giving thanks is an attitude that will change our daily outlook. Remember, *mishpat* means, "God's verdicts as Divine Judge regarding the actions of people with one another." Refuse to worry and fret about someone getting by with something. God is always righteous in His judgments.

Father, I rise to thank You for all that You have done for me. I place my trust in You and all of Your righteous judgments. Lord, wake me through the night as You deem fit.

63 I am a companion of all them that fear thee, and of them that keep thy precepts [piqqud].

People often under estimate the importance of having the right people in your life. It's been said that you will become the average of the five people you spend the most time with. Consider how that applies in your life? Are the top five godly people who fear and reverence the Lord? If not, you are shortchanging yourself. Of course, this applies only to the choices that we have. If you have an unbelieving spouse, Paul wrote that you should continue with him/her, unless they opt out (1 Corinthians 7). But when it comes to hanging out with friends and taking advice from others, maintain a high standard. "He who walks with wise men will be wise, but the companion of fools will be destroyed" (Proverbs 13:20).

Lord, help me to choose my friends based on Your criteria, not mine. Surround me with godly people who reverence You. In the multitude of counselors, there is safety and I need that kind of support to be my very best for You.

---

64 The earth, O Lord [Yahweh], is full of thy mercy: teach me thy statutes [choq].

So often the question is asked, "Why does God allow bad things to happen to good people?" Actually, the whole premise of the question is false. The real question should be: why does God allow good things to happen to anyone? The Bible says that there is no one righteous, no not one (Romans 3:10). The earth is full of God's mercy, yet Satan would try to point out pain and suffering that he is responsible for and get people to blame God. Ask God today to teach you His statutes.

O Lord, You are wonderfully perfect in every way. Forgive me for the times I've questioned Your love. The earth is full of Your mercy. Without You, we cannot draw another breath. I pray Lord that You would teach me Your statutes.

Day 9

Teth

65 Thou hast dealt well with thy servant, O Lord [Yahweh], according unto thy word [dabar].

God is much better to us than we deserve. He will always watch over and honor His Word in the lives of His children. The phrase *according unto thy word* speaks volumes. It's important to know what God's Word says about every situation. Of course, the Bible doesn't answer every question that can be asked. However, it does provide direction into every area of life that requires guidance for godliness.

Lord, thank You for Your continual goodness in my life. I am saved by grace through faith and not because of any works I've done. Watch over Your Word and perform it in my life.

_____

_____

_____

66 Teach me good judgment and knowledge: for I have believed thy commandments [mitsvah].

Good judgment. There seems to be a lack of this attribute. I'd like to say that it's only a modern problem. After all, that's our tendency – to embellish the 'good old days.' No, good judgment has always been at a premium. The source to obtain this wonderful quality is the Word of God, and a relationship with its Author. A great place to obtain good knowledge and judgment is the book of Proverbs. There are 31 chapters so it makes a perfect daily devotional. Just read the chapter that corresponds to the day of the month, each day. All of God's Word is good for knowledge and sound judgment. Dive deep and often into the treasures of the Word.

Holy Spirit, You are my teacher. You live within me and are able to personally tutor me at my level. I open my heart to Your instruction. Make me teachable Lord and help me to not only understand Your Word, but to believe it with my heart.

---

67 Before I was afflicted I went astray: but now have I kept thy word [imrah].

Affliction is part of life. In many ways we must learn to differentiate between *life* and God. God is always fair, but life, on the other hand, is often not. The word affliction implies being humbled. Humility always opens the door for greater blessing. There are times when God cannot get our attention and He must use the harshness of life to arrest us. David was a man who knew affliction first-hand, even though he had the anointing of God on his life. Here, he acknowledges that all of the adversity that he experienced was ultimately used by God to keep him from going astray. What are you facing in your life today? God is at work. When we are in the affliction, we so desperately need to hear God's spoken Word to our hearts. Open the Bible today and let God speak to you.

Father, thank You that You not only saved me, but You are also keeping me. Be involved in every facet of my life to keep me in the center of Your will. Keep me humble through the various afflictions of life. I trust You will all my heart.

---

68 Thou art good, and doest good; teach me thy statutes [choq].

What a declaration! Simple. True. God is good! Take time to remember His goodness today. Jesus taught us that *only* God is truly good (Luke 18:19). This verse also reveals a principle found throughout the Bible: *being* precedes *doing*. God is good; therefore, does good. This dynamic is true in all spiritual matters. In order to *do*, one must first *be*. The psalmist is ever asking God to teach him His statutes. Once a person stops learning and growing, life grinds to a halt. Strive to ever be increasing in your knowledge of the Lord.

Father God, I praise You for Your goodness. In all things You are good and all Your deeds are good. Help me to always walk in gratitude for all that You do for me. Teach me Your statutes and help me to continue to learn and grow in my journey with You.

---

69 The proud have forged a lie against me: but I will keep thy precepts [piqqud] with my whole heart.

Once more we see "the proud" being positioned as the enemy. Those who hate God are also inspired to hate God's people. Church Leaders are of special interest to the proud. We know that we do not wrestle with flesh and blood. Satan is the real enemy (Ephesians 6:12). But he uses people and lies against us can be hurtful. Satan's objective is to get you in the flesh and to react presumptuously. Instead, purpose in your heart to abide in God's Word and let the Lord fight your battles for you.

Jesus, the proud hated You and they hate me too. I want to fire back so badly, but instead I put my trust in You. Take me deeper into my relationship with You through all of this. I want to know the power of Your resurrection and the fellowship of Your sufferings.

---

70 Their heart is as fat as grease; but I delight in thy law [torah].

This is referring to the proud (v 69). It says that their heart is as fat as grease. The NIV renders it: "Their hearts are callous and unfeeling." In other words, don't expect them to feel convicted and guilty about their actions. In this case, really all you can do sometimes is to forgive them and move on. Pray that their hearts would turn to God, but until that happens, they will continue to be insensitive. Instead of getting caught in Satan's trap, the psalmist instead delighted in the law of God. The Lord will always have a word in season for those who turn to Him.

Lord, protect me from the proud and hateful. They don't know You or Your ways. I choose instead to walk in love and to delight in Your Word.

---

71 It is good for me that I have been afflicted; that I might learn thy statutes [choq].

The psalmist just mentioned in verse 67 that he was going astray until he was afflicted. With what, we do not know. Here again, he sees the silver lining and acknowledges that in the midst of his affliction God has brought good from it. So much in life is about how we *respond* to the adversities that happen. When it comes to discerning whether a test is from God or from the devil, I have learned the following: God tests our strengths in order to advance us and the devil tests our weaknesses in order to fail us. In the process of affliction, God teaches us His Word in a deeper way.

Lord, teach me Your Word in the midst of my affliction. Help me to keep my eyes on You. I choose to see Your goodness in the situation. You are faithful and I know that You are making a way of escape.

72 The law [torah] of thy mouth is better unto me than thousands of gold and silver.

Those who don't esteem God's Word to be greater than riches have never truly tasted the Word of God. There is no greater education than the one that comes from Divine Scripture. Just consider the book of Proverbs and all the wisdom contained therein about business, relationships and other life matters. There are 31 chapters in Proverbs, which makes it a perfect daily devotional at one chapter per day.

Thank you Father for Your Word. While I once pursued money as if it were the most important, I now know that Your Word is the main thing. Help me to apply it in my life today.

Day 10

 י

Yodh

73 Thy hands have made me and fashioned me: give me understanding, that I may learn thy commandments [mitsvah].

The starting point in relationship with God is to acknowledge that we are made by Him and for His glory. He is the Potter and we are the clay (Romans 9:21). This speaks to His continuing involvement throughout our lifetime. When we become marred, He makes us again as it is pleasing to Him (Jeremiah 18:4). Without God granting, we would have no understanding at all of God's Word. The natural mind cannot process the divine thought of holy inspiration (1 Corinthians 2:14). We continue to learn throughout our lifetime. There is so much wealth in the Word that it is impossible to mine it all out in a million lifetimes. Ask the Holy Spirit to be your teacher.

Dear Lord, thank you for making me in Your image. Use me throughout my lifetime to bring glory to Your name. Make me again and again as it is pleasing to You. Grant unto me understanding of Your Word through the indwelling Holy Spirit.

74 They that fear thee will be glad when they see me; because I have hoped in thy word [dabar].

The people that we surround ourselves with are so important for the long-term success of God's plan for our lives. Whether in ministry or business, we need God's favor and blessing. If we will purpose to do things God's way – that is, according to His Word, He will put the right people in our lives. Those who fear the Lord will be glad when they see you. If the people that you want to be glad are not, then perhaps they are not the ones that God has sent. There is great joy and gladness when you find the team of people that God has assigned to your life.

Heavenly Father, thank You that I am sent by You to do Your work. Surround me with the right people – those who will be glad when they see me. I hope in Your Word alone O God.

75 I know, O Lord [Yahweh], that thy judgments [mishpat] are right, and that thou in faithfulness hast afflicted me.

God's judgments or verdicts are always right. We see things through the optics of our own limited knowledge. But God sees everything and always does what is right for us. This may, at times, include afflictions. The word for *afflictions* (*anah*) simply means "to chasten" or "to humble." Many people assume that affliction always means some type of physical infirmity. This is not the case. God's methods of chastening are varied for sure, but they are always done in love (Hebrews 12:6).

64

Thank You for Your faithfulness O Lord. There are so many things I don't understand. But what I do know is that all of Your judgments in my life are correct and that Your discipline of me is in love. Thank You Jesus.

---

76 Let, I pray thee, thy merciful kindness be for my comfort, according to thy word [imrah] unto thy servant.

Our Father is full of kindness – merciful kindness. Just think how much better our days goes when just one person shows us a small gesture of kindness. God's kindness has no end – it is everlasting. The Interlinear translates the word for kindness as "Your merciful covenant loyalty." Be mindful that the word referred to here is the *spoken word* of God. God delights in speaking to His children; we are His sheep and we know His voice (John 10).

Father, I pray for Your merciful kindness to be revealed in my life today, according to all that You have spoken to me through Your Word. I receive Your comfort through the Holy Spirit.

---

77 Let thy tender mercies come unto me, that I may live: for thy law [torah] is my delight.

Consider the tenderness and compassion of God. From the beginning He has desired communion with the ones made by Him in His image (Genesis chapters 1-3). It is through Him that we live – by His tender mercies. The psalmist here declares once more that the *torah* is His delight – the entirety of God's Word. Some people delight in parts of

God's Word, perhaps the promises. But full commitment to God requires a delight in all that God has to say in His Word.

Lord, my prayer is for my life to be filled with Your tender mercies. It is in You that I live and move and have my being. I delight in all that Your Word has to say, Lord.

---

78 Let the proud be ashamed; for they dealt perversely with me without a cause: but I will meditate in thy precepts [piqqud].

One thing that the Bible makes clear with repeated references is that God hates pride. Pride is what caused Lucifer to fall from heaven (Ezekiel 28, Isaiah 14). The outcome of pride will always be shame because God resists the proud, but gives grace to the humble (James 4:6; 1 Peter 5:5). One of the meanings of the word *perversely* is "to falsify." As followers of Christ, you can expect the proud of this world to persecute you and falsify things about you. This can be very painful from an emotional standpoint. But the Bible is clear in how we should respond: *"Blessed are you when they revile and persecute you, and say all kinds of evil against you falsely for My sake. Rejoice and be exceedingly glad, for great is your reward in heaven, for so they persecuted the prophets who were before you"* (Matthew 5:11-12). Remember, *piqqud* means "detailed instructions from the Lord." The reason that Satan uses the proud to persecute you is to get you off of what God called you to do. Keep your mind focused on your assignment and let the Lord fight your battles for you.

God, you surely resist the proud. I rejoice that I am persecuted for Christ's sake. You will bring the enemy's strategy to shame as I trust in You. Instead of wrestling with flesh and blood, I will instead meditate in Your instructions for my life. Thank You Jesus for Your covering on my life.

---

79 Let those that fear thee turn unto me, and those that have known thy testimonies [`edah].

The psalmist understands the importance of surrounding himself with those who fear the Lord. In verse 63, he said that he was a companion of all who fear the Lord. In verse 74, he said that all those who fear the Lord were glad when they saw him. Now, here in verse 79, he prays that God would send unto him those that fear the Lord. Are you surrounding yourself with people who love and reverence the Lord? The psalmist wants to be around people who know God's Word. The Bible says that if you want to be wise, to hang out with wise people, but a companion of fools will be destroyed (Proverbs 13:20).

Father, send into my life those who love and reverence You. Surround me with people who know Your Word.

---

80 Let my heart be sound in thy statutes [choq]; that I be not ashamed.

What a beautiful prayer: "Let my heart be sound in thy statutes." Soundness of heart is the key to spiritual victory. How can one walk with the Lord without soundness of heart? Jesus came to heal the brokenhearted (Luke 4:18). The word *statutes* relates to God's boundaries. It is great comfort to know that His Word establishes the boundaries whereby my heart can remain sound, complete and whole. God protects us through His statutes from the things that wound the soul. To be ashamed also means to be disappointed. It's only when we get outside of God's boundaries for our life that we meet with disappointment.

Father, I welcome Your beautiful boundaries in my life. I understand that they are for my protection. In You, my heart is sound, complete and whole. All of expectations are complete in Your perfect will for my life.

Day 11

Kaph

81 My soul fainteth for thy salvation: but I hope in thy word [dabar].

There is a part of the Christian journey that meets with unfulfilled expectation: *"My soul fainteth for thy salvation."* In other words, God doesn't move on our timetable. This causes us to become weary in a sense. But, more importantly, it drives us to His Word and refines our hope as something greater than the moment. *"I hope in thy Word!"* Refuse to allow the moment to steal your hope from you. Cling to His Word in times of delay or disappointment. In doing so, the temporal nature of the moment will fade and your hope in the Everlasting God will strengthen.

All my hope is in You, Lord. Even in times of delay when I can't see Your hand at work, I know You are present. Your Word is my constant source of encouragement and strength.

_____

_____

_____

82 Mine eyes fail for thy word [imrah], saying, When wilt thou comfort me?

The failing of the eyes is in the sense of straining to see a distant object. Sometimes the promise in God's Word seems so far away. Remember, *imrah* is God's spoken Word to you. It's a personal promise. God's timing is always perfect, but it's difficult for us to see the reasons for God's delays. Noah patiently built the ark; Abraham tarried for his son; Joseph endured the pit and the prison; David lived as a vagabond before taking the crown. In all of the delays that life brings, God has a purpose. Continue to strain your eyes and stay focused on the Word. God's comfort in all your trouble will not fail you.

Lord I believe Your promise even though I may not see any evidence. All my faith is in You. I receive Your comfort and strength into my life today. Fill me up with expectation, Lord. You will come through for me as You always do, right on time.

83 For I am become like a bottle in the smoke; yet do I not forget thy statutes [choq].

Bottles in the east were made of skin and the metaphor is one of a wineskin being dried up by the smoke. Within the Christian walk, there are definitely times of spiritual dryness. Those who say otherwise have not walked long with the Lord. God will permit such times because He wants us to learn to walk by faith and not feelings. In those seasons, cling to the written Word of God. When we are lacking the feeling of His presence it is easy to begin looking for outward signs and confirmations to guide us. But the more sure word of guidance are the statutes of God's Word.

Father, although I may feel dried up, yet I am alive in You. Nourish me today with the daily bread of Your Word. I remind myself of Your wondrous statutes.

_____

_____

_____

84 How many are the days of thy servant? When wilt thou execute judgment [mishpat] on them that persecute me?

In his humanness, the psalmist reminds God that his life is short-lived and transitory. The Hebrew word for judgment (*mishpat)* means, "God's verdicts as Divine Judge regarding the actions of people with one another." Although at times it seems that our persecutors get by with their malicious activities, rest assured that God is in control and vengeance is the Lord's (Romans 12:19). We must resist the urge to self-defend against our persecutors. Continue to allow the Lord to be your defense. In due time, He will respond and He will raise the standard against the enemy's tactics.

Lord, you know my frailties and my weaknesses. I am but human. I put my trust in You alone. You are my defense and my comfort.

_____

_____

_____

85 The proud have digged pits for me, which are not after thy law [torah].

The proud will always be the enemy of God; therefore, they will be the opponents of God's friends. What the devil wants is for you to be so focused on your enemies that you lose sight of what God has called you to do. The psalmist uses this word *proud* (*zed*) five other times in Psalm 119 (21, 51, 69, 78, 122). The reality is that the Bible tells us that we will be persecuted for the Word's sake (Mark 4:17). Refuse to allow the proud of this world to distract you from God's plan.

Father, thank You that in You is all my sufficiency. The proud have dug puts for me, but the Holy Spirit is my guide. You prepare a table before me in the presence of my enemies!

---

86 All thy commandments [mitsvah] are faithful: they persecute me wrongfully; help thou me.

God's commandments (*mitsvah*) express His authority. He is always faithful. The previous two verses also talked about persecution. Over the years, I have seen that persecution comes in all different forms. But we are to draw encouragement from God's Word, no matter the type of persecution we're facing. The fact that it is being done wrongfully gives us cause to rejoice. "Blessed are you when they revile and persecute you, and say all kinds of evil against you falsely for My sake. Rejoice and be exceedingly glad, for great is your reward in heaven, for so they persecuted the prophets who were before you" (Matthew 5:11-12).

Lord, I rest in Your faithfulness. Your authority reigns supreme in my life. All my persecutors have wrongfully accused me, but my help is in You. I resist the urge to self-defend and instead allow You to fight my battles. Help me, Lord.

87 They had almost consumed me upon earth; but I forsook not thy precepts [piqqud].

The psalmist's persecutors had almost consumed him. The word for *consumed* (*kalah*) means "spent or finished." The key word is *almost*. God will not allow you to be tested beyond your ability to overcome (1 Corinthians 10:13). In the middle of adversity it is imperative that you do not forsake the Word of God for your life. Remember, *precepts* (*piqquid*) means, "Detailed instructions from the Lord." Refuse to get off mission and become absorbed in the drama that goes along with persecution. This is the devil's objective. Just because God's word for your life is being tested does not mean it will fail to come to pass. What is needed is for you to cling to that word and trust the Lord.

O God, you know my true status. I am almost consumed, but I am still here because of Your grace. It is because of You that I do not forsake your word and plan for my life. Strengthen my faith today, Lord.

88 Quicken me after thy lovingkindness; so shall I keep the testimony [eduth] of thy mouth.

The word *quicken* means "to make alive." God is our continuous source of life. His covenant stipulations (*eduth*) are not designed to punish us or make life less fulfilling. The basic agreement in a covenant is that *everything you have belongs to your covenant partner and everything your covenant partner has belongs to you*. This is quite the magnificent transaction for man: all that God has! But the stipulation requires all that we have. God requires full commitment to His Word and His ways. Even the word for *lovingkindness* (*checed*) in my Interlinear is translated "covenant loyalty." It is because of God's covenant loyalty that we are not consumed and continue to be refreshed by His Spirit.

Lord, You are a covenant-keeping God. You watch over Your Word to perform it. Quicken me in Your loyal and everlasting kindness. Help me, O God, to keep my part of this great covenant by giving You all of me.

_____

_____

_____

Day 12

Lamedh

89 For ever, O Lord, thy word [dabar] is settled in heaven.

As we begin day 12 of our devotional, we come upon one of my favorite verses in the Scripture. In a world around us that is filled with change, there is one sure constant – God's Word. It is forever settled in heaven. When dealing with the uncertainties of life, the Word brings us assurance that God is in control. Jesus said, "Heaven and earth will pass away, but My words will never pass away" (Matthew 24:35). Many people throughout time have attempted to change or alter the Word of God. While some have done so to their own ruin, the pure, unadulterated Word stands as sure today as ever. When you have a need, find the corresponding promise in the Scriptures and apply it by faith. God has not changed and neither has His Word.

O Lord, I rest in the eternal and unchangeable Word of God. I apply Your truth to every facet of my life. Though the circumstances may change, Your Word is forever settled in heaven Lord and I trust You in every way.

90 Thy faithfulness is unto all generations: thou hast established the earth, and it abideth.

Verse 89 speaks of heaven and verse 90 of earth. This verse does not contain one of the nine Hebrew words that are translated as a form of Scripture. It does, however, speak of God's faithfulness. God has a testimony in all generations, starting from Adam until the modern period. We know that in the fullness of time, God sent forth His Son (Galatians 4:4). The Father is always on time and He is always faithful to His promise.

Father, thank You for Your complete and unfailing faithfulness in my life. You are my constant source of strength and encouragement. I will continue to depend on You all the days of my life.

91 They continue this day according to thine ordinances [mishpat]: for all are thy servants.

The *they* mentioned at the beginning of the verse is in reference to heaven (v. 89) and earth (v. 90). Heaven and earth are under God's jurisdiction. His ordinances and judgments cause everything to be upheld. "All are thy servants" means that the worlds – both heaven and earth, obey His commands. Everything is subject to His authority.

Lord, You are Lord of all. Every knee shall bow and every tongue confess that You are Lord. Thank You that You are in control.

92 Unless thy law [torah] had been my delights, I should then have perished in mine affliction.

What a powerful testimony! Afflictions are inevitable, even for the believer. The word for *affliction* simply means *trouble*. Jesus warned us that in this life we would experience trouble, but He also told us to be joyful because He'd overcome the world (John 16:33). All of God's Word – the entirety of His instruction is valuable throughout life's troubles to draw us closer to God and give us the proper perspective. Without the beautiful insights of the Word of God, we, like the psalmist, would be overwhelmed by our afflictions. Child of God, in your times of trouble, cling to the Word of God. It will surely be a lamp unto your feet and a light unto your path (119:105).

Father, in all my afflictions I look to You. My delight is found in Your Word. I refuse to let my faith waver in my difficulties. Instead, I will rejoice for You have overcome the world Jesus.

93 I will never forget thy precepts [piqqud]: for with them thou hast quickened me.

Forgetfulness of God's Word is a great error among God's people. The book of Deuteronomy alone is filled with admonitions to not forget God and His Word (4:9, 23, 25-31; 6:10-12, 14-15; 8:10-14, 19-20; 9:7-8; 11:18-20; 12:29-31; 16:1-3; 18:9-13; 31:24-27). However, it is within human nature to forget – to be more focused on the current problem than the faithfulness of God. This is why we must continually remind ourselves of God's promises and all that He has done for us in the past. As the psalmist states, with His Word, He quickens us or makes us come alive. So many times in the past I have been discouraged and God used His Word to bring strength and courage into my heart.

Thank You Lord for Your faithfulness in my life. Your precepts are my source in all my ways. Through them you continually strengthen me.

---

94 I am thine, save me: for I have sought thy precepts [piqqud].

What beautiful words: "I am thine." Child of God, know this, you are His. Never forget this because He will never leave you. His promise is that He will not leave you as an orphan (John 14:18). His precepts are His detailed instructions. There are times when God is seemingly silent. Yet He instructs us to seek Him. In doing so, He reveals Himself. It is especially important to remember His detailed instructions when we find ourselves in difficult or adverse situations. The enemy can shoot fiery darts at our mind to get us discouraged and to question God. When that happens, hold on dearly to what He has told you. God is faithful to both keep you and to fulfill His Word.

Father, I am thine. My trust is in You. I thank You that You have given me Your Word and though I am tested for the Word's sake, you will save me.

---

95 The wicked have waited for me to destroy me: but I will consider thy testimonies [edah].

The enemy of our souls is perpetually in a mode of waiting, unless of course, he has sprung to attack. The Bible says that when Satan had ended his tempting of Jesus that he departed from Him for a *more opportune time* (Luke 4:13). The enemy never gained an advantage with Jesus – as He was sinless. The power of the Holy Spirit and the knowledge of God's Word are also able to keep us from falling. Not, of course, that we will be sinless. But He will empower us to live a holy life. The NASB translation uses the words "diligently consider" in this verse; to be diligent is to be thorough and persistent. It is crucial to press in during times of temptation or testing. Doing so will strengthen the soul as well as get us safely to the other side.

Lord, though the enemy waits to destroy, You have already defeated him on the cross. I do not fight to get to the victory, but from the place of victory. I will diligently consider all that Your Word declares.

---

96 I have seen an end of all perfection: but thy commandment [mitsvah] is exceeding broad.

What the psalmist here is saying is that even perfection has its limits, but the Word of God has none. It is measureless and unlimited. There is no bottom to the Book. I have been studying God's Word for over 35 years and I learn something new every day. There are passages that I have read hundreds of times and yet the Spirit will reveal something to me within the text that I've never seen before. From a king's viewpoint, David had seen many beautiful things, but nothing compared to the matchless beauty and perfection of God's Word. God's commandments are so broad that they are pertinent and useful in every situation and in every generation, without exception.

O God, Your Word is truly beyond perfection in that nothing in this world compares. Lord, continue to reveal to me the hidden gems of Your precious truth.

_____

_____

_____

Day 13

Mem

97 O how love I thy law [torah]! it is my meditation all the day.

The purpose for this devotional book is to inspire people to fall in love with God's Word. The psalmist said that it was his meditation all the day. When you are in love, the object of your love will consume your thoughts throughout the day. Psalm 119 speaks much about the reverence we are to have for God's Word, but additionally we are to have a heartfelt affection for the Scriptures. The torah is the entirety of God's Word. In other words, we are not to love just portions of God's Word, but all of His instruction.

Lord, teach me to love Your Word. Throughout my day bring to my remembrance the precious truths You have revealed to me.

---

98 Thou through thy commandments [mitsvah] hast made me wiser than mine enemies: for they are ever with me.

Our knowledge of God's Word must go beyond *head knowledge* or an intellectual understanding. Spiritual knowledge is revealed to a believer by the Holy Spirit. This is what the New Testament describes as the "sword of the Spirit" in Ephesians 6:17. On our own we are no match for the devil, but through the Word of God we are made wiser than our enemies. Satan knows the written Word, but he has no revelation knowledge as he is cut off from the Spirit of God.

Thank You Lord that You have made me wiser than my enemies through Your Word. They have no authority over me because greater is He who is in me.

---

99 I have more understanding than all my teachers: for thy testimonies [eduth] are my meditation.

Understanding of God's Word comes from the Holy Spirit, through time spent studying and meditating on the Scriptures. Teachers are part of the process, meaning that God uses them to impart knowledge. But even in the teacher—student relationship, it is the Holy Spirit who reveals truth. If a student is devoted to God's testimonies, there can come a time when he or she has more insight into the Scriptures than the teacher. This is not, however, a source of pride. For when knowledge puffs up (1 Corinthians 8:1), it has clearly not produced authentic revelation into the heart.

Lord, thank You for my teachers; they are a gift into the body of Christ and to my life, personally. But I know that the real teacher is the Holy Spirit; He is my tutor and lives within me. I open my heart to His instruction.

100 I understand more than the ancients, because I keep thy precepts [piqqud].

The psalmist, in this stanza, is emphasizing that God will not withhold knowledge of the truth from anyone who sets their heart to seek Him. He declares that through God's Word, he is wiser than his enemies and has more understanding than his teachers and, here, the ancients. How old a person is has very little to do with how much they know when it comes to the things of God. God reveals truth to those who are hungry. Jesus prayed, "O Father, Lord of heaven and earth, thank you for hiding these things from those who think themselves wise and clever, and for revealing them to the childlike" (Matthew 11:25 NLT). Of course, being old doesn't disqualify one from being wise in the Scriptures. The idea is that regardless of age, God must be sought before He will be found (Jeremiah 29:13).

Lord, I want to grow old with the knowledge of God. I don't have all the wisdom that's needed to succeed in Your plan for my life. Help me to understand Your Word so that I can apply it throughout the years and seasons of my life.

101 I have refrained my feet from every evil way, that I might keep thy word [dabar].

Every day is filled with decisions. Choices are made to either follow God's path or the way of evil. In order to keep God's Word, we must refrain our feet from every evil way. To refrain speaks of abstinence. There are many things that we cannot partake of if we are going to please God. Some of those things don't necessarily appear to be evil, but the Holy Spirit within checks us to refrain. This is the Spirit-filled life.

Lord, thank you for the daily guidance You provide. Even when I don't understand, I trust You Lord. Give me the power to refrain my feet from evil and to keep Your Word.

---

102 I have not departed from thy judgments [mishpat]: for thou hast taught me.

To depart (Heb. *sur*) means to "turn aside, out of one's course." The psalmist trusts in God's verdicts. Things do not always turn out the way we expect or want, but we must trust in Him that He knows what is best. It is common, especially in western Christianity, to "invent" a God in our mind that is different than the God revealed in the Bible. When He doesn't perform according to our expectations it seems that God has failed us. The psalmist declares, "Thou hast taught me." If we will allow our view of God to be shaped by our study of Scripture and actually view life through the lens of God's Word, we will never turn aside or depart from His judgments.

Father, I trust You in all Your judgments in my life. I see only what's in front of me, but You know all things. Gird me with strength to live this life pleasing to You and not to depart from Your Word.

---

103 How sweet are thy words [imrah] unto my taste! yea, sweeter than honey to my mouth!

It has been said that the Bible is a love letter to His children. It is much more than that, but in many respects, this is true. Taste speaks of personal experience – inward revelation. *Imrah* is the spoken word of God, similar to the Greek word *rhema*. When the Holy Spirit speaks to you out of the Scripture and makes it personal for you, it is very much like tasting God's Word for yourself. There is nothing that can quench the thirst of the soul more than a word in season from God. It is sweeter than honey to the taster.

Father, Your Word is my delight. It is sweeter than honey to my mouth. The words of human wisdom never satisfy, but Your Word satisfies my soul.

---

104 Through thy precepts [piqqud] I get understanding: therefore I hate every false way.

When you discover your purpose in God it will make you hate every false way. God's *piqqud* is His detailed instruction for our lives. One of the greatest aspects of living for God is the knowledge that there is divine destiny and purpose at work in your life. Without this understanding, the feeling of being left to one's own devices can be devastating. Proverbs 14:12 says, "There is a way that appears to be right, but in the end it leads to death." The Hebrew word for *false* (*sheqer*) means deception, disappointment and falsehood. Satan always has a counterfeit for God's perfect will. Don't allow yourself to be deceived. Allow His Word to give you understanding.

Lord, Your ways are above my ways and Your thoughts are above my thoughts. Give me understanding into Your detailed instructions for my life and teach me to hate every false way.

Day 14

Nun

105 Thy word [dabar] is a lamp unto my feet, and a light unto my path.

Without the illumination of the Word of God, we will wander off the path that God has placed us on. As people, our tendency is to stray. The carnal nature is estranged from God and wants to figure out its own way. But the new nature embraces the light and direction that comes from God's Word. It must be remembered that this path is traveled one step at a time. Further, it is often God's method to only reveal the next step without full disclosure as to where it will lead. We must trust Him in all our ways and He will direct our paths (Proverbs 3:5-6).

Lord Jesus, I need the light of Your Word shining in my life. Direct all my ways and help me to line up to your Word in all the areas that really matter.

106 I have sworn, and I will perform it, that I will keep thy righteous judgments [mishpat].

To *have sworn* is to have solemnly promised in the form of an oath, with God as your witness. People often make commitments to God without follow-through. It's easy to promise God certain things when we want something from Him. It's our way of *creating leverage* while the problem is ongoing. The truth is that God sees the intent of the heart. But there are still times when God will grant the request out of His mercy. Jesus taught us to let 'yes' be 'yes' and our 'no' be 'no' (Matthew 5:37). In other words, don't make commitments that you aren't going to keep. If you have made a solemn promise to God that you will keep His Word, follow-through and keep your promise.

Father, I pray that You would help me to keep my commitments. By Your help, may my 'yes' be 'yes' and m 'no' be 'no.'

---

107 I am afflicted very much: quicken me, O Lord [Yahweh], according unto thy word [dabar].

There are numerous occasions in David's life when he was afflicted. Psalm 34:19 says, "Many are the afflictions of the righteous: but the LORD delivereth him out of them all." But even in affliction the Lord is able to revive (quicken). Why does the Lord allow these afflictions into the lives of His followers? One reason is to drive us to His Word. There's no way of knowing what type of affliction the psalmist was experiencing, but it was not beyond the reach of a loving God. Whatever type of trouble may be in your life today, know that God is in control. Place your trust firmly in Him and cling to His Word.

Jesus, You know my troubles and You see my affliction. Without You I can do nothing. All my ways are before You. Lead me and revive me by Your Spirit.

---

108 Accept, I beseech thee, the freewill offerings of my mouth, O Lord [Yahweh], and teach me thy judgments [mishpat].

Our praise is an offering with which the Lord is always pleased. We must be willing to accept His verdicts in life. We may not understand everything or even agree, using our finite comprehension, but we trust in the Lord and know His dealings are just. The only offerings from the mouth that the Lord accepts are those that come from the heart. Jesus scolded the Pharisees because they honored God with their lips, but their hearts were far from God (Matthew 15:8).

Lord, I offer to You the sacrifice of praise, the fruit of my lips. Thank You that all of Your judgments are true and just. I trust You in every aspect of my life.

---

109 My soul is continually in my hand: yet do I not forget thy law [torah].

The New Living Translation of this verse states, "My life constantly hangs in the balance, but I will not stop obeying your instructions." David frequently found himself in some perilous situations. King Saul tried to kill him no less than 12 times. Many of the psalms were written at a time when David's life was hanging in the balance. Yet this one thing he did – he remained faithful to the Word of God.

God's instructions apply to every moment of life. There is no situation where God does not have applicable wisdom in the Holy Scriptures. Remind yourself of what God has to say in His torah and encourage yourself in the Lord.

Lord, though my life may hang in the balance, yet will I trust in You and follow Your instructions. Speak to me through Your Word.

---

110 The wicked have laid a snare for me: yet I erred not from thy precepts [piqqud].

The conspirators of evil in the kingdom of darkness frequently and strategically lay snares for the children of God. Of course, we realize that the whole world system is under the influence and sway of the evil one (1 John 5:19). But Jesus did not pray that we would be taken out of the world but that we'd be protected from the evil one while in the world (John 17:15). Piqqud is the detailed instructions from the Lord. These are of great importance when navigating around a snare. Satan is subtler than any enemy known to mankind (Genesis 3), but God's revelation is always greater than any strategy of the devil. If God has given you particular instructions, don't deviate from them.

Thank You Father for Your detailed instructions for my life. The enemy has tried repeatedly to trip me up and distract me from Your will. But I will not err from Your precepts.

---

111 Thy testimonies [eduth] have I taken as an heritage for ever: for they are the rejoicing of my heart.

A heritage is a valued object that is inherited. The psalmist saw the Word of God as his treasure. All that is in the atmosphere and the earth will fade away, but God's Word will endure forever (Matthew 24:35). God's testimonies (eduth) are tied to His covenant and His covenant is eternal. For the New Covenant to fail, Jesus would have to fail since He is the One who cut it with the Father on the cross. Rejoice today in knowing that Jesus will never fail and that God is watching over His covenant in your life to uphold it.

Father, I embrace Your covenant word in my life. It is greater than all riches. I have taken it as my heritage and I will rejoice in knowing that Jesus will never fail.

112 I have inclined mine heart to perform thy statutes [choq] alway, even unto the end.

There is an inclination from the Holy Spirit that gets engraved into our hearts to perform God's statutes. The word *choq* carries with it the idea of engraving or inscribing. Philippians 2:13 (NLT) says, "For God is working in you, giving you the desire and the power to do what pleases Him." This determination to keep God's Word must be set to endure – even unto the end. If every choice were easy, life would be simpler. But there are difficult decisions to be made and crossroads to confront. Make a bold decision today to do it God's way.

Thank You Holy Spirit for inscribing the Word of God on the tablet of my heart. Today, I choose to follow the Word in every aspect of life – unto the end.

_____

_____

_____

Day 15

Samekh

113 I hate vain thoughts: but thy law [torah] do I love.

The word *vain* (Heb. *seeph*) can also be translated *divided* or *halfhearted*. I heard the late David Wilkerson say once, "Balance was a code word for a divided heart." We must guard our hearts that we don't "balance" ourselves right out of the will of God. Vain thoughts will attempt to focus on self and the preservation of our personal interests. Loving God's Word means making decisions that align with the Scripture and renewing our mind to the truth of God on a daily basis. After an individual has spent a considerable amount of time meditating in the Word, vain thoughts are identified and recognized as an enemy that must be cast down (2 Corinthians 10:5).

Jesus, I set my mind on You and fix my heart on Your Word. Help me to guard my mind against vanity and the emptiness of this world's allurement.

114 Thou art my hiding place and my shield: I hope in thy word [dabar].

Quiet time with the Lord is all about the hiding place. Our devotional time with God is a place of solitude and rest. Notice that David says, "Thou art my hiding place." It is the Lord Himself that is our hiding place. It is not a service for Him or a blessing from Him, but He Himself is our refuge. Hope is something of which the world knows very little about and has even less of. But as followers of Jesus, we hope in His precious Word! It isn't about seeing how many chapters you can read each day, but instead allowing God's Word to build strong roots into your life – your affections, your decisions and your behaviors.

Lord, You alone are my hiding place and fortress of rest. Touch me today with Your sweet presence and fill me with Your joy. I have hope because of You and Your wonderful promises. Thank You Jesus.

---

115 Depart from me, ye evildoers: for I will keep the commandments [mitsvah] of my God.

Spiritual authority must be exercised in the advancement of God's purposes in the earth. The believer has been given the use of the name of Jesus, which has all authority in heaven and in earth (Matthew 28:18). Wherever God's will is being done there will always be opposition from the enemy's camp. When Jesus was tempted by the evil one (Matthew 4, Luke 4), He used the Word of God to defeat the devil. Mitzvah signifies God's authority. We must remember that there is great authority with the Word. God always watches over it to perform it (Jeremiah 1:12) when we choose to keep it.

Father, as I walk in Your will there are many opponents. I pray that You would remove the evildoers and help me to keep Your commandments with all my heart.

---

116 Uphold me according unto thy word [imrah], that I may live: and let me not be ashamed of my hope.

God will sustain His children through the power of His Word. He will not allow us to sink under the weight of our burdens. There is a hope that comes from the Word of God that allows us to have supernatural hope in the absence of natural hope. This was Abraham's case. Romans 4:18 says, "Who, contrary to hope, in hope believed, so that he became the father of many nations, according to what was spoken, 'So shall your descendants be.'" Imrah is God's spoken Word. Abraham had a spoken Word from God to him personally and he was able to be strong in hope until the promise was fulfilled. Allow God to speak to you today and give you a cheerful, confident expectancy.

Lord God, sustain me by the power of Your Word. May I live out all of Your purposes for me and never be disappointed in my hope in You.

---

117 Hold thou me up, and I shall be safe: and I will have respect unto thy statutes [choq] continually.

Where would we be if God didn't uphold us throughout life's many turns and troubles? One of the ways God upholds us is through setting boundaries in His Word. The word *choq* means, "God's regulations and boundaries for His people, individually and collectively." When we try to live our lives outside of the boundaries of God's Word, we expose ourselves to all sorts of danger – physically and spiritually. When, instead, we have respect for God's statutes, nothing is able to subvert His plan in our lives. The Hebrew word for *respect* (*shaah*) means, "to keep in our constant gaze." Whatever you may be going through, keep your eyes on Jesus and have respect for His statutes.

Father, thank You for all the times You have upheld me and delivered me from danger. Help me to keep my gaze continually upon Your statutes and trust You at all times.

---

118 Thou hast trodden down all them that err from thy statutes [choq]: for their deceit is falsehood.

When people stray or wander from God's statutes, the Lord will reject their efforts. As the prophet Samuel said the King Saul, "To obey is better than sacrifice" (1 Samuel 15:22). When we substitute our best in place of God's best, we are fooling ourselves. *There is a way that seems right to a man, but its end is the way to death* (Proverbs 14:12). There will be times when God's ways do not make sense to the natural mind. In those moments, we must bear down and trust in God's wisdom above our own. To think that we can take matters into our own hands and defy God's statutes is deceitful and vain.

Dear Lord, put a tremble of reverence and awe in my heart for Your statutes. I will not choose my own way, but will trust in the Lord with all my heart.

_____

_____

_____

119 Thou puttest away all the wicked of the earth like dross: therefore I love thy testimonies [edah].

For a season, dross may be mixed with gold or some other precious metal. This does not make it valuable by association. Ultimately, it will be discarded as useless. All of the wicked were created in the image of God with the opportunity to choose God's plan of redemption. There is nothing of value in any of us apart from God, but through the miracle of the new birth we are made precious in His sight. _Edah_ speaks of covenant. When we enter this wonderful covenant relationship with the Father, His testimonies become our delight.

Thank You Lord that You have chosen me for Your family and I am precious in Your sight. Remove the dross of my life – those things that are unnecessary for Your plan for me.

_____

_____

120 My flesh trembleth for fear of thee; and I am afraid of thy judgments [mishpat].

We should never get too casual with God lest we take His name in vain or fail to hallow His name. God is holy and though His children, we must be mindful to fear the Lord. Proverbs tell us that the fear of the Lord is the beginning of wisdom (Proverbs 9:10). His judgments and verdicts must be revered. Everything God does is perfect.

Lord, may Your name be hallowed in my life through all that I say and do. I have an awe and reverence for Your presence and Your Word. Make me holy just as You are holy.

_____

_____

_____

Day 16

Ayin

121 I have done judgment [mishpat] and justice: leave me not to mine oppressors.

The psalmist says that he has done what the Word instructed him to do. The Bible says "don't judge" in Matthew 7:1, but this is in reference to our own self-serving judgment. The Bible outlines for us the meaning and use of *righteous judgment*. When we are judging from a self-serving position we can never help our brother get unstuck (Matthew 7:5). If you do things the right way by following the Word, you will not be left to your oppressors. Proverbs 16:7 says, "When a man's ways please the LORD, he makes even his enemies to be at peace with him." The temptation is to setup a wall of self-defense when we are attacked or slandered, but God's wisdom says to just keep focusing on pleasing the Lord and let Him fight your battles.

Lord, You are the righteous judge and know all things. I trust in Your judgment. Help me to align my decisions and attitudes with Your will. Deliver me from my oppressors.

122 Be surety [arab] for thy servant for good: let not the proud oppress me.

In verse 122 we have an instance where one of the nine Hebrew words for the Scriptures is not used. Instead, the psalmist uses the Hebrew word *arab*, which is translated *surety*. David sees God's Word as a guarantee and implores God to uphold His pledge. The Lord always keeps His promises. He watches over His Word to perform it (Jeremiah 1:12). And all that God does is good; every good and perfect gift is from the Father (James 1:17). This is the sixth and final time David mentions "the proud" (Heb. *zed*) in Psalm 119. This verse is a prayer of spiritual warfare, asking God to drive back the proud oppressors. For the New Testament believer, these are demonic spirits, as we do not contend with flesh and blood (Ephesians 6:12).

Thank You Father that You are the only guarantee I need as You always keep Your Word. I trust You to drive back the enemy in my life and bless me with every good and perfect gift.

123 Mine eyes fail for thy salvation, and for the word [imrah] of thy righteousness.

The psalmist's eyes were failing, or being strained, looking and longing for the deliverance that only God could provide. The salvation mentioned here is the temporal kind, not the eternal. David looked for God to breakthrough in his situation and deliver him out of his troubles. There will be season in our walk with God when it feels that God has forgotten us. But God is always faithful and is true to His Word. If you have an *imrah* from God (the Old Testament equivalent of *rhema*), stand on it until you see the salvation of God.

Lord, I so desire to see you work in my life and bring deliverance and wholeness in my heart. Help me to see the need for personal change and not just a change in the circumstances. I love You Jesus.

---

124 Deal with thy servant according unto thy mercy, and teach me thy statutes [choq].

God's mercy is His unfailing love. God always deals with His children according to His mercy. That is not to say that all of God's dealings are pleasant. The Word tells us that the Father chastens those whom He loves (Hebrews 12:6-11). God knows how to perfectly balance His mercy with His correction to bring our lives into adjustment with His will. To the believer that is seeking to follow Jesus, every situation is an opportunity for the Lord to teach us His statutes – His regulations and boundaries. For the superficial believer, God's boundaries are something to circumvent; loopholes are sought for to escape the Lord's constraints. But the sincere follower understands that God's boundaries are setup for our protection and done so in tender love.

Father, I submit to You and all Your dealings with me. I know that they are done in love. Except for Your mercy I would have perished in my affliction. Teach me Your statutes through it all, Lord.

101

125 I am thy servant; give me understanding, that I may know thy testimonies [edah].

The Hebrew word for *servant* is *ebed* and is referring to a bondservant. This was a special type of servant that had the legal right to go free but instead chose to stay and serve his master out of love, for life (Exodus 21:5-6). This is the type of service we are to offer our Lord – all to be done out of love for Him. We should serve, however, with discernment pertaining to His will. There are many "good" things that we can help with and serve, but we should pursue those things that are from God. Doing good things will never change the world, but dong God things will have an eternal impact. God's testimonies will provide the direction we need to make a difference.

Lord God, I choose to be Your bondservant for life. I love You with all my heart and will never leave You. Give me understanding of Your will for my life and help me to know Your testimonies.

---

126 It is time for thee, Lord [Yahweh], to work: for they have made void thy law [torah].

I've often said that *God takes a long time to do things suddenly*. The point is that God has perfect timing and there is always a purpose in what we deem to be a delay. The world around us has made every effort to make God's Word *void*. This word means to "cast off." While some of God's Word is still being accepted, it is the *entirety* of His Word (torah) that is rejected. So as society continues to spiral downward in a post-Christian culture, God's people are anticipating the last great outpouring of the Holy Spirit. These are the last of the last days and God will fulfill His promise of revival (Joel 2:28-32). Jesus always saves the best wine for last!

It is time, Lord! Pour out Your Holy Spirit and move in our midst. Empower us to be light to this darkened world.

---

127 Therefore I love thy commandments [mitsvah] above gold; yea, above fine gold.

More than anything, I want this devotional book to inspire a love affair with the Word of God. I spent months praying these verses every night and God used that to flood my heart with revelation knowledge of Him through His Word. To love God's Word more than gold speaks to priorities. Jesus said that we couldn't serve both God and money (Matthew 6:24).

Lord, I love Your Word above all that is material. Grant me revelation of Yourself through the treasures of Your Word.

---

128 Therefore I esteem all thy precepts [piqqud] concerning all things to be right; and I hate every false way.

God's ways are higher than man's. His instructions for living don't answer every curious thought or solve every mystery. But we are given everything we need to be victorious and live a godly life. The world is filled with false ways and counterfeits. But those counterfeits are difficult to discern when you don't know the truth. Counterfeit experts are trained by performing intense scrutiny of the genuine article, not by studying the counterfeits. Once a person knows the truth of God's Word, it is easy to identify the fake. Paul wrote, "Test everything and hold fast to what is good" (1 Thessalonians 5:21).

Lord, I know all of Your precepts are perfect and right concerning everything in my life. Expose every false way and deceptive strategy from the devil.

_____

_____

_____

Day 17

Pe

129 Thy testimonies [eduth] are wonderful: therefore doth my soul keep them.

God's Word is wonderful and extraordinary. A student could spend a lifetime and in the process become a scholar, but still just be scratching the surface of the depth of God's Word. It's my prayer that you are not only reading and praying God's Word in this devotional journal, but also tasting the Word of God and delighting in its wonder. God's commandments are not burdensome (1 John 5:3). Allow yourself to fully submit to God's testimonies. Embrace them with your whole heart.

Father, Your Word is wonderful and I long for more understanding so that my soul can be fed and I can continually practice Your truth.

_____

_____

_____

130 The entrance of thy words [dabar] giveth light; it giveth understanding unto the simple.

The entrance of God's Word gives light! The word for *entrance* (Heb. *pethach*) means "the unfolding." When God's Word gets unfolded in our lives there is so much clarity that happens. It isn't that all of *your* questions get answered, but your perspective changes in that you begin to see things how God wants you to — with an eternal viewpoint. The word for *simple* means to be open-minded. If a person is not open-minded, very little understanding will be given. Unfortunately, within the church world, people are told what to believe and question very little of it. Pray that God would give you a teachable spirit and an open mind in order to receive understanding of His Word.

Father, Your Word gives me light to see. Without it I have no direction. Make my heart teachable and give me an open mind to know and understand Your truth.

---

131 I opened my mouth, and panted: for I longed for thy commandments [mitsvah].

To open your mouth and pant speaks of desire and thirst. Many have very little appetite for the Word of God. There's a good chance that since you are reading this devotional that you have a hunger for the Word. When God sees this in one of His children, He always feeds them with revelation knowledge. God will feed you based on your ability to comprehend and apply. New Christians receive the milk of feeding on the meat of the Word — deeper truths (Hebrews 5:14). No matter where you are, God has something for you if you desire to be fed with His Word.

Lord, You placed a desire inside me for Your Word. I long for Your commandments. Feed me with Your truth.

---

132 Look thou upon me, and be merciful unto me, as thou usest [mishpat] to do unto those that love thy name.

The psalmist beseeches God to look upon him and to be merciful. We always have God's loving attention, but there are times when we *feel* a distance or estrangement from His presence. Of course, this is the error of human emotion, but the feeling is real nonetheless. In these times, like the psalmist, we cry out to God to look upon us. In His tender mercy, He obliges with the warmth of His presence. *Mishpat* is normally translated as *judgments*. God's judgments and God's name is perfectly aligned. To be unfair or imbalanced in His judgments would be a reflection on His name. When we love His name we are also agreeing with His judgments.

Dear Lord, look upon Your servant and be merciful to me. All of Your judgments are righteous and Your name is holy and true. I love You Jesus.

---

133 Order my steps in thy word [imrah]: and let not any iniquity have dominion over me.

The Word of God and the Holy Spirit are in perfect and complete harmony and agreement. No one can claim to be led by the Holy Spirit while doing that which is contradictory to the Scriptures. *Imrah* is the spoken Word of God, which means the Holy Spirit uses the

Word of God to speak directly and personally to our hearts. God wants to order our steps in this supernatural way. When we are walking in the freedom of the Holy Spirit and aligning our lives to the Word of God, sin has no control over our lives. Pray today for God to order your steps in His Word and to break the control of sin from your life.

Dear Lord, order my steps and my life according to the Word of God. Speak to me through the Scriptures. Bring me into total victory over sin, for Your glory.

---

134 Deliver me from the oppression of man: so will I keep thy precepts [piqqud].

The word oppression carries the idea of cruelty or control that is *prolonged*. Christians can find themselves in a state of oppression through neglecting to keep on the whole armor of God (Ephesians 6). Oppression is a condition where a person wants to be free but feels powerless to bring it about. In the psalmist's case, oppression was coming in the form of man, but for the New Testament believer, our battle is with the unseen forces of darkness (Ephesians 6:12). God is able and willing to deliver the child of God by His Spirit. Only from a place of freedom are we able to keep God's precepts – His detailed instructions. Meanwhile, Satan the oppressor seeks to abort the plan of God for your life. Draw near to God and resist the devil and he will flee from you (James 4:7).

Father, please deliver me from the oppression of the enemy. I want to live out Your perfect plant for my life.

---

135 Make thy face to shine upon thy servant; and teach me thy statutes [khoke].

God's face shining on his servant represents His favor. Numbers 6:25 says, "The Lord make His face shine upon you, and be gracious to you." Walking in God's favor is such an advantage in this life. There is nothing we can do to *earn* His favor, but there is a direct correlation between His statutes and His blessing and favor. Remember, *statutes* carry the idea of boundaries. We will only have God's favor when we walk within His boundaries. If you feel that your life is lacking the favor of God, ask Him to reveal His statutes to you and help you to walk in them.

Thank You Lord that You shine Your face upon Your servant. I praise You for the kindness and blessing You bestow. Teach me Your statutes and boundaries as I walk this life of faith.

136 Rivers of waters run down mine eyes, because they keep not thy law [torah].

The psalmist weeps tears of sorrow because God's people have turned their backs on His law. This reminds me of Jeremiah, known as the weeping prophet. Jeremiah 13:17, "But if you will not listen, my soul will weep in secret for your pride; my eyes will weep bitterly and run down with tears, because the LORD's flock has been taken captive." While David was zealous to keep God's law, his heart was deeply broken that others dishonored the Torah.

Father, break my heart with what breaks Yours. Fill my heart with a longing to see Your people obey Your Word.

_____

_____

_____

Day 18

Tsadhe

137 Righteous art thou, O Lord [Yahweh], and upright are thy judgments [mishpat].

Righteousness, as seen in the Old Covenant, is primarily related to ethical conduct. The Lord (Yahweh) is always fair and ethical in all His conduct. In the New Covenant, the child of God is the recipient of the imputed righteousness of God – 2 Corinthians 5:21 *For He made Him who knew no sin to be sin for us, that we might become the righteousness of God in Him.* Through the washing of the blood, righteousness is credited to our account before God. God's judgments are always straightforward, just and right.

Thank You Lord for imputing to me the righteousness of God, in Your unfailing love. Your judgments in my life are always just and fair.

---

138 Thy testimonies [edah] that thou hast commanded are righteous and very faithful.

God sets forth His covenant stipulations (edah) in His Word for a purpose. All that God does is righteous and faithful. He never deviates from His protocol set forth in Scripture. Yahweh is bound to His covenant and desires to bless His people more than they desire to be blessed. God never asks more of us than what we are able to do through His power in us. His commandments are not burdensome (1 John 5:3).

Dear Lord, thank You so much for Your testimonies; they guide me through the storms of life. Your instructions are always righteous and faithful.

---

139 My zeal hath consumed me, because mine enemies have forgotten thy words [dabar].

The word for *zeal* (Heb. *qin'ah*) denotes strong passion. Of the 43 times it is used, it is most often translated *jealousy* (25 times). Benson's Commentary states, "Zeal is a high degree of love; and when the object of that love is ill treated, it vents itself in a mixture of grief and indignation, which are sufficient to wear and consume the heart." It is only God's people that can forget God's Word; unbelievers know neither God nor His Word. Guard your heart that you do not forget God's Word in times of blessing when He may seem less needed in your life.

Father, my prayer is to hold onto Your words and to be consumed with a zeal that keeps my passion for You strong. It breaks my heart that those who knew You have forgotten Your words.

---

140 Thy word [imrah] is very pure: therefore thy servant loveth it.

The word for *pure* (Heb. *tsaraph*) means "to be tested." The NIV translates this, "Your promises have been thoroughly tested…" Imrah is the Hebrew equivalent of the Greek word *rhema*, meaning "God's spoken word to you." When the Holy Spirit speaks a word to you, know this, His word is very pure and has been tested. No matter how impossible the promise may seem, God will make it happen if you have faith. Luke 1:37 (NIV) says, "No word (rhema) from God will ever fail." Choose to love God's promise by reminding yourself daily that God is working and the breakthrough is coming.

Lord, You have proven Your Word over and over throughout the ages and in my own life. It is very pure and I love Your promises. I will stand on Your Word when times get the hardest and have faith in You.

141 I am small and despised: yet do not I forget thy precepts [piqqud].

God chose the weak and foolish things of this world to confound the wise and mighty (1 Corinthians 1:27). When David was chosen by God to be King over Israel, he was the youngest and the least of Jesse's sons (1 Samuel 16). He was despised by his brothers and considered too unimportant by his father to present to Samuel. But God looks on the heart, not the outward appearance (1 Samuel 16:7). God had a perfect plan with detailed instructions for David. He is the same God to you and wants to lead you with His precepts.

Father, thank You that You have chosen me and set Your love upon me. Though I may be unimportant in the world's eyes, I am not to You. I will remember Your precepts and follow them all my days.

---

142 Thy righteousness is an everlasting righteousness, and thy law [torah] is the truth.

The righteousness of God is unchanging. He is always upright in all of His dealings. Under the Old Covenant sin wasn't fully dealt with. God instituted a system of animal sacrifices to atone for sin, but the blood of bulls and goats could never remove sin. Everything pointed to the cross. When Jesus was crucified, He vindicated the righteousness of God (Romans 3:25-26). Before the cross, God was forbearing. But on Calvary, His wrath was poured out on sin (past, present and future) when His Son became a sin offering that we might be made the righteousness of God in Christ (2 Corinthians 5:21). God's Word is the truth that will make us free (John 8:32).

Thank You Jesus for taking my place on the cross. Your righteousness is everlasting and unfailing. There is no other truth than the truth of Your Word.

---

143 Trouble and anguish have taken hold on me: yet thy commandments [mitsvah] are my delights.

David understood what it was like to have trouble and anguish. The Hebrew word for *trouble* (*tsar*) means, "narrow or tight." The pressures of life can squeeze upon a child of God and cause great anguish. But here, David reveals the secret to overcoming those seasons of life. He chose to delight in the Word of God instead of focus on the problem. God's commandments are His absolutes and in times of confusion and distress it is good to know that there are established boundaries to keep you from danger.

Lord, the pressures of this life have gripped me, but in response, I choose to grip Your Word even tighter. I will delight in the safeguard of Your boundaries.

---

144 The righteousness of thy testimonies [eduth] is everlasting: give me understanding, and I shall live.

Knowing that all of God's ways are right and *understanding* them are two different things. Understanding comes from the Holy Spirit. He is the one who gives us the spirit of wisdom and revelation in the knowledge of Christ (Ephesians 1:17). Jesus told us that if we know the truth, the truth would make us free (John 8:32). I often say that it's not the truth that makes us free, but the truth that we *know* that makes us free. Jesus came that we might have abundant life (John 10:10), but there's no way for that to happen if we remain ignorant of His Word. "God's people are destroyed because of a lack of knowledge" (Hosea 4:6).

Father, Your Holy Spirit is the one who gives me understanding. I open my heart to Your testimonies.

Day 19

Qoph

145 I cried with my whole heart; hear me, O Lord [Yahweh]: I will keep thy statutes [choq].

There's something about seeking the Lord with your whole heart. Personally, I know when I'm seeking with a distracted heart or a divided heart. It's the times when I am seeking with my whole heart that I feel closest to the Lord. The Hebrew word for *whole* (*kol*) also means, "to avoid stiffness." Jeremiah said, "You will seek me and find me, when you seek me with all your heart" (Jeremiah 29:13). Keeping God's statutes when your heart is not in it is simply outward performance. It's only when we obey him from the heart that we are truly blessed.

Lord, with my whole heart I cry out to You and seek Your face. May Your will be done in my life and Your name be glorified. Help me to keep Your statutes.

146 I cried unto thee; save me, and I shall keep thy testimonies [edah].

The theme of verse 145 is carried over here. To cry out to the Lord is an act of the heart. The Lord's ears are open to our pleas. Here the psalmist implores God to save him. Throughout Psalm 119, David makes his heart known and never shies away from divulging his predicaments. He knew that God was the only one who could deliver him out of his troubles. Personally, I try to live by the principle of never sharing my problems with those who have no ability to help solve them. This means, they will pray for me, encourage me or offer good advice to help solve the problem. First and foremost, the one to turn to in times of trouble is the Lord. *Edah* speaks to covenant relationship. Our problem is the Lord's problem. His testimonies are our source of guidance.

Dear Father, I cry unto You because You alone are my source of strength. Deliver me from snares of the enemy and help me to keep Your testimonies.

---

147 I prevented the dawning of the morning, and cried: I hoped in thy word [dabar].

There is something special about rising before dawn to seek the Lord. Putting God first in your day allows your life to be aligned to His purposes for your life. Throughout the book of Psalms, the psalmist refers to rising early to seek God. Jesus Himself would often withdraw from the disciples before dawn to spend time with the Father (Mark 1:35). The only way that one can have true hope in the Word is to spend time in it. We live in a very hopeless world and often when we start our day without the Word, the negativity around us eats away at our hope. Decide today to get built up in the hope of God's Word before you face your day.

Lord, I purpose in my heart to spend more time with You and in Your Word. Help me to rise earlier and to put You first in my day. I truly hope in Your Word.

---

148 Mine eyes prevent the night watches, that I might meditate in thy word [imrah].

Not only does the psalmist rise before the dawn to cry unto the Lord, he also frequently stays up through the night. Desperate times call for extreme measures. Here, David speaks of meditating or reflecting on God's promises. If you don't guard your heart, the devil will keep you up all night to worry about the problems of tomorrow. Instead, choose to meditate in God's spoken promises to your life. Often we are permitted by God to experience these tests and trials in order to drive us to our knees. Trust in the Lord and His plans.

Lord, wake me through the night as You see fit. Stir my heart with Your great and precious promises. I will meditate in Your Word.

149 Hear my voice according unto thy lovingkindness: O Lord [Yahweh], quicken me according to thy judgment [mishpat].

Perhaps there is nothing more consoling than knowing that Almighty God – Yahweh hears our voice. Often, when we are struggling with a matter and confide in someone, our true desire is not for advice, but instead to be heard. Our Father in heaven meets that need. He not only listens, but does so according to His lovingkindness. He is a compassionate listener. Unlike human help that is often limited or unavailable, God is able to move in the situation. He wants to make you alive again and restore you according to His Word.

O Lord, hear my voice today and know my heart. You are always compassionate and loving. Revive me and stir me according to Your Word.

---

150 They draw nigh that follow after mischief: they are far from thy law [torah].

Persecution often comes from people who have no real interest in serving the Lord, even though they may attend church. These people continually find themselves in some form of mischief, but it isn't coincidental, as they'd have you believe. The word for *mischief* (*zimmah*) means "planned wickedness." They always *draw near* those who are making the most impact for the Kingdom in order to cause distraction and disruption. Be careful who you surround yourself with, that you may guard the mission that God has given you.

Lord, You know all my persecutors and You alone are my defender. These people are far from Your law. I pray that their hearts would be repentant and they'd turn to You for mercy.

151 Thou art near, O Lord [Yahweh]; and all thy commandments [mitsvah] are truth.

Even though persecutors may draw near us with malicious intent, the Greater One – Yahweh is ever so near to protect us. The name Yahweh is only for His covenant people – those with whom He's in relationship. The New Testament says, "The person who is joined to the Lord is one spirit with him" (1 Corinthians 6:17). He cannot deny you, for to do so would be to deny Himself. Yahweh does, however, set forth commandment as guard rails to keep our lives from derailing. All of His commandments are truth, and the truth will make you free (John 8:32), not bind you up.

Thank You for Your continual presence in my life Yahweh. I gladly accept all of Your commandments into my life.

---

152 Concerning thy testimonies [edah], I have known of old that thou hast founded them for ever.

"I have known of old," means that the psalmist has a history with God. Time and experience adds an important component to one's spiritual resumé. It is wonderful to know things from a book. This is often the best place to start in the acquisition of knowledge. But depth in the knowledge we have comes about by living the truth through the ups and downs of life. David knew from a very young age that God's Word would endure forever. As he lived, both as a fugitive and a king, his understanding deepened. Whatever you are going through in your life at this moment, know that God's Word is worthy of complete trust.

Lord, teach me Your testimonies and help me to trust You. I know that Your Word will endure forever and You will fulfill every promise in Your Word.

_____

_____

_____

Day 20

Resh

153 Consider mine affliction, and deliver me: for I do not forget thy law [torah].

The Father is attentive to the suffering of His children. Indeed, He considers our afflictions and delivers us in His goodness. When we are going through the suffering it can be difficult to remain positive, but if we will trust God, the process will go much better. The psalmist reminds God that he has not forgotten His law. There are many times throughout life that we must endure great affliction or hardship. In those seasons, God molds us and conforms us into the image of Christ. Everyone wants the power of His resurrection, but we must also embrace the fellowship of His suffering (Philippians 3:10).

Father, look upon my affliction and see my suffering. In Your faithfulness, make a way of escape that I might endure. I do not forget Your Word, which is my source of comfort.

154 Plead my cause, and deliver me: quicken me according to thy word [imrah].

Plead my cause! Some other translations of this statement are as follows: "Defend my cause" (NIV); "Argue my case" (NLT); "Champion my cause" (CSB); "Fight for me" (NET). Self-defense is a terrible strategy. As Christians when we are opposed or persecuted, we must let the Lord fight our battles and defend our case. Once more the psalmist pleads with God to deliver him. This word for *deliver* can also be translated as *redeem*. We are in a blood covenant with God, through the shed blood of Jesus and as such, God will indeed stretch forth His hand to deliver. He will quicken or revive us according to His Word. God always keeps His promises so look to the Lord in your affliction today and call on His name.

Lord, I trust You completely to defend me when I am attacked. Deliver me, as You've always done. Revive me according to Your Word.

---

155 Salvation is far from the wicked: for they seek not thy statutes [choq].

Jesus said that the road that leads to destruction is very broad (Matthew 7:13). Satan has a way of deceiving the masses with the appeal of popularity or fortune or some other attraction. The further down the road to destruction, the more removed the wicked are from salvation. But it's never too late to call on Jesus for deliverance. Choq represent God's boundaries and the wicked see no need for boundaries to keep them from their wicked pleasures. But God is only trying to prevent the certain destruction that is coming when one chooses against God's will.

Lord, I pray for the lost all around me. They are so far from You and live in rebellion to your Word. Open their eyes and save them Lord.

---

156 Great are thy tender mercies, O Lord [Yahweh]: quicken me according to thy judgments [mishpat].

Yahweh's tender mercies surround us and are greater than any negative force that comes against us. Jesus, Yahweh in the flesh, ministered to people from the motivation of compassion. He was trying to prove who He was. In fact, many times He told those He healed to not tell anyone. Jesus loved people and still does. Whatever you're going through right now, just know that His tender mercies are upon you. He will revive you according to His perfect verdicts. Don't be fooled by the appearance of evil winning for it is only temporary. The Lord will restore – even sevenfold (Proverbs 6:31).

Thank You Yahweh for Your great compassion towards me. I'm so undeserving but eternally grateful for all You do. Revive me and use me for Your glory.

---

157 Many are my persecutors and mine enemies; yet do I not decline from thy testimonies [eduth].

When you are in covenant with God, He will fight your battles for you. Sir Henry Morton Stanley, the famous Welsh explorer to Africa in the 1800's ultimately cut covenant with over 50 African tribes. Whenever he was faced with an enemy he would show the scars from those covenant cutting ceremonies and the enemy would immediately retreat. Stanley's enemies knew that to fight him would be to fight those 50 tribes. Remember, child of God, when someone comes against you, they are coming against God Himself, for you are the apple of His eye (Zechariah 2:8). The English Standard Version renders the past part of the verse, "I do not swerve from your testimonies." Do not allow your persecutors to cause you to swerve from what God has called you to do. Romans 8:31 says, "If God is for us, who can be against us?"

Lord, I am in covenant with You through the shed blood of Jesus and no matter what comes against me, I know that You are for me. By the power of Your Spirit, I will not swerve from the Word and the call of God on my life.

---

158 I beheld the transgressors, and was grieved; because they kept not thy word [imrah].

The meaning of *transgressors* (Heb. *bagad*) is "the faithless or disloyal." David's heart was broken over others' faithlessness to the Word of God. I counsel with people on a regular basis and one common denominator in dysfunctional lives is the failure to live by the principles set forth in Scripture. God will answer prayer or even do a miracle and shortly thereafter people revert right back to the old way of living. It's heartbreaking because it's dishonoring to God. Let us remember today to not be faithless or disloyal to the One whom we owe everything!

Dear Lord, let my heart break for what breaks Yours. People all around forget You and neglect Your Word. May I always place You first in my life.

159 Consider how I love thy precepts [piqqud]: quicken me, O Lord [Yahweh], according to thy lovingkindness.

What a blessing to have detailed instructions (piqqud) from the Yahweh! Jesus told us that the Holy Spirit would show us things to come (John 16:13). When you walk in close communion with God, it gives the Holy Spirit occasion to speak into your life. I can think of many personal words that the Holy Spirit has given me over the years and I cherish each one. Once more, petition is made for Yahweh to revive the psalmist. Just because you have the Lord's plan doesn't mean that there won't be a battle. Paul told Timothy, "This charge I entrust to you, Timothy, my child, in accordance with the prophecies previously made about you, that by them you may wage the good warfare" (1 Timothy 1:18 ESV). When God gives you a word, know that it will be tested and there will be times when the Lord needs to revive you.

Thank You so much Yahweh for the precious Word and instructions You've given me. I hold them dear. Revive me according to Your lovingkindness.

160 Thy word [dabar] is true from the beginning: and every one of thy righteous judgments [mishpat] endureth for ever.

Every word from God ever spoken is true. Many versions translate this first statement as, "The sum of Your word is truth." Every single word is true and the sum of all His words is true. *All*

Scripture is given by inspiration of God, and is profitable for doctrine, for reproof, for correction, for instruction in righteousness (2 Timothy 3:16). God's Word endures forever, thus it is relevant for every generation. When God speaks through His Word, it is a timely message from the timeless truth of His Word.

Thank You Father for Your eternal Word. I receive the timeless truth of Your Word into all aspects of my life.

_____

_____

_____

Day 21

Shin

161 Princes have persecuted me without a cause: but my heart standeth in awe of thy word [dabar].

One of the most difficult challenges in life can be when persecution comes without a cause. People can use very hurtful words in an effort to disrupt your progress in the Lord. The term "princes" would refer to anyone in authority. It is especially arduous when the persecution comes from those in authority or leadership. In those situations, one thing I try to do is examine my heart to see if there is any verity to what is being spoken, even if it's being said with the wrong attitude. The natural inclination is always to self-defend, but the mature thing to do is to allow the Lord to fight your battle. Frequently, the entire goal from the adversary with the persecution is to distract us from the mission and get our eyes off Jesus. Instead, fear the Lord and stand in awe of His Word.

Lord, even when I am persecuted I remain in awe of Your Word. You are my defender and my shield. I trust in You, Jesus.

162 I rejoice at thy word [imrah], as one that findeth great spoil.

It's my prayer that through this devotional you will find the Word of God to be a great treasure. There is a *finding* aspect to the study of the Scriptures that makes the exercise so rewarding. Every day, the Holy Spirit brings something new to light. It might be a verse you've read a hundred times, but this time the Holy Spirit speaks to you or show you a nugget that you'd never seen before. Don't ever believe the notion that you can't understand the Bible. You have a tutor who lives within you – the very One who wrote it!

Thank You Father for the many great treasures I find in Your Word. Open my eyes to see more as I spend time with You.

163 I hate and abhor lying: but thy law [torah] do I love.

Jesus plainly told us that Satan is the father of all lies; lying is his native language (John 8:44). God's law is the truth. One would think that everyone hates being told a lie, but the reality is that some people don't mind a lie if it makes them feel better about themselves. Sometimes the truth hurts in the moment, so instead people seek out those who will tell them what they want to hear. God said through Jeremiah, "The prophets prophesy lies and my people love it this way." Of course, verbal lying is the most known method of lying, but Satan uses other forms as well. Anything that contradicts God's law is a lie. These lies can come in the form of circumstances or symptoms. While some of these conditions may indeed be factual, if they contradict God's law they are lies.

Lord, I hate and abhor every type of lie. I only want the truth in my life – the truth according to You. Close off every source of lies in my life and lead me into all truth.

---

164 Seven times a day do I praise thee because of thy righteous judgments [mishpat].

David was very intentional about his worship. He never took the attitude that he would praise God whenever he was in the mood. In one place, he wrote that he would do it evening, morning and noon (Psalm 55:17). In another place, he wrote that he would do it at midnight (Psalm 119:62). It's important to develop daily habits of praising God. Whether the seven here is literal or figurative (seven represents perfection), it is clear that the psalmist prioritizes his time with God. Specific to the reference here are God's righteous judgments. Sometimes when people are persecuting you, there is a need to keep reminding yourself that God's verdicts are fair and just. Praising God is a great way to do this.

Father, thank You so much for Your righteous judgments. I set my heart to be deliberate and intentional is praising You.

---

165 Great peace have they which love thy law [torah]: and nothing shall offend them.

This verse has been a constant source of inspiration for me over the years. There is so much that we can get offended over in today's world. In fact, getting offended has become a fulltime occupation for some. But if we truly love God's law, He will keep us in perfect peace and nothing will offend us. Now, surely offense will try to come, but if we allow God's Word to take root in us, there will be no place for a root of bitterness. It is impossible to have peace while at the same time being offended. A person has to decide which one they want to rule their heart. The Bible describes the peace of God as a garrison that protects our hearts and minds (Philippians 4:7). If you allow it, God's peace will protect you. Choose to walk in forgiveness and refuse to be offended.

O Lord, You bring my peace through Your Word and it protects my heart and mind. I choose not to be offended today, no matter what comes my way.

---

166 Lord [Yahweh], I have hoped for thy salvation, and done thy commandments [mitsvah].

Bible hope is not the same thing as the hope that's expressed through modern language. The latter is more of a wish and the former is a cheerful, confident expectancy. As followers of Christ we live with a hope inside our hearts that can't be extinguished by circumstances or disappointments. Salvation in this verse is referring to deliverance. God will make a way of escape (1 Corinthians 10:13). The devil attacks the believer's hope because without hope, faith has no target, for faith is the substance of things hoped for (Hebrews 11:1). Stir up the hope of God in your heart today and commit to walking by faith.

My hope is in You Yahweh. Though life may not seem fair and circumstances may be hard, You will make a way for me as I practice the truth of Your Word.

167 My soul hath kept thy testimonies [edah]; and I love them exceedingly.

Not only did David keep God's testimonies outwardly, but he did so from the passion of his heart. Keeping God's Word will ultimately result in a test. There will be times when it's more convenient to take a shortcut or make a compromise. Choosing instead to keep doing it God's way will bring great blessing. Here, the psalmist expresses his sheer delight in God's testimonies. Once you make up your mind to follow God's Word, there is pure joy in being a doer of the Word. However, many Christians opt instead to use an *introductory trial period* approach. In other words, I'll give it a try but reserve the right to go back and do it my way if I'm not getting the results I like. Decide today that you will keep God's Word in all situations and in every season of life.

Father, I choose to be a doer of the Word of God. My mind is set and my heart is fixed. I delight in Your Word, O God.

168 I have kept thy precepts [piqqud] and thy testimonies [edah]: for all my ways are before thee.

The psalmist kept, or obeyed the detailed instructions (piqqud) given him. Those instructions, of course, are tied to His covenant stipulations or requirements (edah). Together, they frame up the will of God for our lives. Some want a set of instructions that are separate from the requirements given, but God doesn't operate that way. Further, David declares, "All my ways are before thee." This means God knows the ins and outs of our existence – what we have and don't have. If the Lord has given you instructions to do something, He full well knows the resources you have. His intention is for you to trust Him in every area you come up short. We serve a God of abundance and He is absolutely devoted to meeting the needs associated with His will.

Father, all my ways are before You and You know all my limitations. I choose to trust in You and obey Your instructions for my life. Help me to live within the conditions You've set.

_____

_____

_____

Day 22

Taw

169 Let my cry come near before thee, O Lord [Yahweh]: give me understanding according to thy word [dabar].

Yahweh is very in tune with the cries of His people. If you remember, it was the cries of Israel in Egypt that prompted Him to send Moses to deliver them (Exodus 2:23-25). The Lord stores all of our tears in a bottle (Psalm 56:8). In emotional times, it can be difficult to have clear understanding of God's Word for our lives. Special attention should be paid to removing barriers to that understanding. I've discovered that trying to make major decisions during times of duress can be hazardous. Spend extra time in prayer and also going back over the direction God has given you in the past. Allow the peace of God to rule in your heart as you mediate on His Word.

Yahweh, hear my heart's cry. I need You in my life at this moment. Please break through and show Yourself strong. Give me clear and certain understanding and direction from Your Word.

_____

_____

_____

170 Let my supplication come before thee: deliver me according to thy word [imrah].

Supplication is to make a petition for God's favor. When making such petitions, we do so with both humility and confidence. Humility because we remember our status as the creation – weak and dependent upon Him. Confident because we know what has been promised us as joint heirs with Christ. This is David's tact here in verse 170, "Deliver me according to thy word." The NIV translates *word* as *promise*. If we do not know God's promises, wherein is our faith? Our needs and sorrows touch the heart of God, but it is our faith that moves the hand of God.

Father, help me in my weakness. Grant me favor in Your kindness. I put You in remembrance of Your promise and thank You in advance of my deliverance.

---

171 My lips shall utter praise, when thou hast taught me thy statutes [choq].

The New Testament describes the praise for God that's on our lips as a sacrifice. *By him therefore let us offer the sacrifice of praise to God continually, that is, the fruit of our lips giving thanks to his name* (Hebrews 13:15). Choq represents God's boundaries, which we must be taught. Our selfish orientation, the flesh, does not like to be denied. But if we have a willing heart to learn and grow, God will indeed teach us His statutes. Sometimes it's a trial and error experience and we have to endure the Lord's correction, but He always deals with us in love. It is better to be corrected by one who loves you than to be praised by fools. Begin to offer praise to God that He loves you enough to shut certain doors that are not His will. Unless God shuts the wrong doors, you will never get to the right one – the door of promotion from God.

Lord, I offer to You the sacrifice of praise – the fruit of my lips. So many times I thought I was going the right way but You loved me enough to save me from myself. Teach me Your statutes, O Lord.

---

172 My tongue shall speak of thy word [mitsvah]: for all thy commandments are righteousness.

Almost every other translation uses the word *sing* in place of *speak* in this verse. The English Standard Version translates it, "My tongue will sing of your word." Singing God's Word is one of the great ways to learn and memorize the Scripture. The human brain was designed with a great capacity towards musical influence. Often we get part of a song stuck in our head just by hearing it at the grocery store or in the car – even if we don't like the song. One major pitfall in much of today's worship music is the lack of sound theology as its underpinning. If we aren't careful, we'll find ourselves singing about all sorts of things at church instead of sound biblical lyrics. Be intentional when you sing praise to God, to use Biblical phraseology and ideology.

Lord, I speak and sing of Your Word. Let it pour forth abundantly from my heart. All of Your commandments are perfect in every way.

---

173 Let thine hand help me; for I have chosen thy precepts [piqqud].

When problems arise, the wise veteran of spiritual battles will turn to the Lord for help. Trusting in the arm of the flesh will always prove futile. A wise person once said, "Don't tell your problems to anyone who doesn't have the capacity to help you solve them." That's good wisdom to live by. This trusted individual might have resources, guidance or only prayer support. As great as timely help is when it comes through these avenues, our real and lasting help comes from the Lord. Put your faith in God and listen to His instruction. God will send the right people, even if they appear to be the wrong ones at first. Elijah had to wonder how a widow was going to provide for him when she was preparing her last meal with what little she had left (1 Kings 17). God will provide when you obey His precepts – His detailed instructions.

Lord, You alone are my source. You may use others to help, but I know that it is ultimately from Your hand. Help me to hear Your detailed instructions and obey them, even when they don't seem reasonable to my natural mind.

---

174 I have longed for thy salvation, O Lord [Yahweh]; and thy law [torah] is my delight.

As people, we long for those things that are our delight. This almost goes without saying, but sometimes it's not so obvious. People who say they love the Word of God, but spend very little time reading it are being insincere. I have discovered that the more time I spend in the Word, the greater desire I have to come back. I believe you've read through this devotional because you have a desire to know

Yahweh and His Word better. I stand in agreement with your prayer and believe that Yahweh will open your eyes to great revelation out of His Word. I pray that your desire will grow stronger and that your discipline will be firm as you continue to pursue Him.

Yahweh, I long for Your presence and Your salvation. I ask You for a stronger desire to read and study Your Word. Make it my delight O Lord.

---

175 Let my soul live, and it shall praise thee; and let thy judgments [mishpat] help me.

God's judgments are His rules. Whoever said that Christianity didn't have any rules didn't read his Bible. The point is that His rules actually help us instead of weighing us down. Here, the psalmist understands the grand objective of life: "Let my soul live and it shall praise thee." Our purpose in living is to bring God praise. This final stanza in the psalm has much to say about the importance of praise. When we gather as a church, praise is not a warm-up act to get us ready for the sermon. God inhabits the praises of His people (Psalm 22:3). The Lord wants to meet with us during the act of praise and worship. When your very existence is in jeopardy, as David's was here, offer to God the sacrifice of praise. The praises that costs the most, counts the most.

Father, thank You for Your judgments; let them help me in my adversities. I offer to You the sacrifice of praise.

---

176 I have gone astray like a lost sheep; seek thy servant; for I do not forget thy commandments [mitsvah].

The psalmist brings us back to a somber reality as he closes this beautiful psalm – our tendencies are no better than a lost sheep. Life is filled with obstacles and challenges that will try to steal the Word of God out of our hearts. At times, it may appear to have succeeded. But know that God never leaves you or forsakes you (Hebrews 13:5). He is the Great Shepherd and when we are lost, He will leave the ninety-nine and bring us back. When you put the Word of God into your heart, it will not return void. The Holy Spirit will bring it to your remembrance when you need it the most. As you have completed this devotional study of Psalm 119, I encourage you to go through it again, or just use the Bible and read through and pray Psalm 119 for a continued season of your life. The rewards are out of this world!

Dear Lord, thank You for this amazing journey through Psalm 119. Often, I wander astray and need You to bring me back. Continually remind me of Your Word and help me to complete this journey here on earth for Your glory.

Books by David Chapman

The Fullness of the Spirit
Modern Day Apostles
The Pattern and the Glory
Thus Saith The Lord
The Power of the Anointing
Knowing God's Will
The Power of Praise
The Seven Letters of Jesus
Caught Up
Blood Covenant
The Believer's Deliverance Handbook
The Kingdom Within
Overcoming Life's Enemies
Counted Faithful
Unlocking the Power of Honor
Thy Word

You can send David an email at TheRiverAZ@gmail.com